A PARENT'S GUIDE TO

Tutors and Tutoring

A PARENT'S GUIDE TO

Tutors and Tutoring

How to Support the Unique Needs of Your Child

James Mendelsohn, Ph.D.

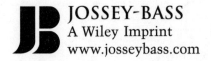

JOSSEY-BASS
A Wiley Imprint
www.josseybass.com

Published by Jossey-Bass
A Wiley Imprint
989 Market Street, San Francisco, CA 94103-1741—www.josseybass.com

Jossey-Bass books and products are available through most bookstores. To contact Jossey-Bass directly call our Customer Care Department within the U.S. at 800-956-7739, outside the U.S. at 317-572-3986, or fax 317-572-4002.

Jossey-Bass also publishes its books in a variety of electronic formats. Some content that appears in print may not be available in electronic books.

Library of Congress Cataloging-in-Publication Data

Mendelsohn, James.
    A parent's guide to tutors and tutoring : how to support the unique needs of your child / James R. Mendelsohn.
        p.   cm.
    Includes bibliographical references and index.
    ISBN 978-0-470-25383-0 (pbk.)
        1.   Tutors and tutoring.   2.   Children with disabilities—Education.
    3.   Remedial teaching.   4.   Education—Parent participation.   I. Title.
    LC41.M46   2008
    371.39'4—dc22

                                                                    2008018987

Printed in the United States of America
FIRST EDITION
PB Printing   10 9 8 7 6 5 4 3 2 1

CONTENTS

For Philip Simmons and John Binder

ACKNOWLEDGMENTS

THIS BOOK would have been impossible without the suggestions, advice, and insights of others. The faults of the book are mine, the strengths of it the result of many.

I am especially grateful to Doctors Deirdre Barrett, Lisa Goldfarb, Brunhild Kring, Stephanie Lesk, Reji Mathew, Pamela Meersand, and William Tucker. The list does not end there: Sam Abrams provided significant insight and unwavering support. Rose Mendelsohn rose to the occasion with a winning suggestion. Dr. Barbara Kravitz helped in so many ways that I can only begin to acknowledge her here. I am grateful for the invitation to speak and thereby test my ideas before the clinicians at the Counseling and Behavioral Health Division of the New York University Student Health Center.

My agent, Judith Riven, was indispensable at virtually every stage, clarifying my confusions, bolstering my determination, and otherwise teaching me how to see this book into being. My editor, Alan Rinzler, was invaluable, first for seeing the possibilities of this book, second for his patience with me, and third for his careful and expert editorial guidance. I thank as well other members of the staff of Jossey-Bass/Wiley, including Nana Twumasi, Mary Garrett, Jen Wenzel, Natalie Lin, Andrea Helmbolt, Jeff Puda, Carrie Wright, and Marcy Marsh for their hard work in producing this book.

Finally and foremost, I thank the parents and students with whom I have worked these past eight years. They continue to tutor me.

A PARENT'S GUIDE TO

Tutors and Tutoring

To Tutor or
Not to Tutor

You've bought this book for your own good reasons. You want to know more about tutors and tutoring, specifically about whether your child needs tutoring. Welcome to a community of similarly concerned parents who have the same questions.

Across the nation, tutoring has become a white-hot issue for families and educators, increasing in importance every day. The evidence that tutoring has become a social and educational phenomenon is overwhelming. In 2005 alone, the United States spent $4 billion on tutoring, only $250 million of which was assumed by public school districts. That leaves $3.75 billion, spent mostly by parents. As these numbers show, tutoring is now perceived as a common if not essential part of education.

Parents like you have turned to tutors out of increasing concern, real and imagined, appropriate and ill advised, for the education of your children. That concern is more than the common anxiety about whether a child's individual needs are being met by a school. Many of you worry that your children may not flourish in an increasingly competitive world, that they may not achieve financial security or social success if they don't get good grades, if they don't get into the right college, if they don't perform flawlessly once there. You may worry that their opportunities will shrink, raising the real possibility that they will lead less happy or comfortable lives than you do. What parent would not have these concerns in such a competitive world?

Such concerns have led many parents to exhibit a hair-trigger response to any sign of "difficulty" that their child might exhibit at school. You hear repeatedly that education is in crisis. You hear teachers and students complain that the testing requirements of the "no child left behind" law have forced your school to focus its curriculum on preparing kids for standardized tests: it crowds out the development of critical and creative thinking; it takes time away from all the subjects—music, art, and phys ed—where your child's interests and intelligence may flourish.

You know the number of hours that your child spends studying is far greater than when you were in school. You see the pressures your child faces to perform. And at the same time, you hear powerful and persuasive advice from education experts, such as Howard Gardner and Robert Sternberg, for everyone to recognize and nurture the varieties of intelligence in students—to educate students "one mind at a time," as pediatrician Mel Levine has declared. If not, they say, your child's unique mind won't be appreciated, and worse yet your child's talents may go undeveloped and his or her life consequently stalled.

In such an environment, it's no wonder that parents like you turn to tutoring as a vital part of meeting what you feel is a desperate need. Each of you has a unique child with a distinct educational situation. But here are some of the typical problems that lead you to consider tutoring:

- You feel you have a responsibility to "make my thirteen-year-old child smarter" so he can compete for spots in the best secondary and high schools, as well as get into the best colleges or universities.

- You feel your high school student *must perform* exceptionally on the PSAT, SAT, or ACT, because they are crucial in the competition for admission to the Ivy League and to other elite schools.

- Your twelve-year-old daughter is doing well in one subject but not in another.

- Your thirteen-year-old son has been diagnosed with *attention deficit disorder* (ADD) or *attention deficit hyperactivity disorder* (ADHD), and you're under pressure from the school or local doctor to put him on Ritalin or another prescription medicine so he'll stay seated at his desk and behave himself quietly in the classroom.

- Your fifteen-year-old has poor study habits, which may be related to ADD or ADHD but might also be developmental or gender based, demonstrating a kind of restless or kinetic style of learning.

- Your four-year-old has been diagnosed as somewhere on the spectrum for *autism disorders*, from mild to severe, and is having problems communicating and socializing in his classroom.

Parents have a difficult choice to make: Should you tutor your child? Will it further your child's ability to learn? Are you helping or hurting your child's development?

Let's take a closer look at these typical problems. Let's consider them as general categories and see how they relate to your needs and your specific questions about tutors and tutoring. For that purpose, I'm going to use stories that are loosely based on my experiences but altered, sometimes significantly, to protect the privacy of actual families and to illustrate the advice this book offers.

Students Whose Parents Believe They Should Make Their Child Smarter

Diane struck me as uncomfortable from the first moment I met her. She was seated on a couch next to her father, while her mother stood facing me—blocking most of my view of Diane. Clearly, Diane's parents felt that she wasn't the one I was supposed to pay attention to at the moment.

"She's just not living up to her potential," Diane's mother declared. Her father nodded his head in agreement.

Diane's mother explained, "She works pretty hard, but she can work harder. She's had straight A's every year of high school, and now, just as she enters her critical high school years, just as she begins to fill out her record for college, she gets a B in AP Chemistry. She needs to do better."

When I asked why they thought Diane should do better, Diane's father chimed in, "It's obvious. She needs to get into a good college."

"She's at a very, very good high school. We made sure of that," Diane's mother added. "We fought hard to get her into the right nursery school and then elementary school . . . we did the same for her middle school. And—AND—we've had her do a summer enrichment program building houses in Guatemala. We sent her on an intensive language-learning trip to Europe and a cultural exchange to Japan. We got her on the best regional girls' soccer team. She played against the top teams around.

"All along, she's had the best," Diane's mother continued. "We even played her those baby Einstein tapes when she was an infant."

"We've set the table for her," Diane's father said. "Now Diane needs to sit down and eat."

In the silence that followed this last statement, Diane's mother must have thought better of her comments. "It's of course not just Diane's problem," she added. "This supposedly great school she goes to—don't get me started!" Diane's father rolled his eyes in agreement. "But Diane needs to do her part. We want you to do that for her."

"We hear good things about you," Diane's father added matter-of-factly.

I asked to speak with Diane privately. Once her parents left the room, I asked her whether she thought she needed to be tutored.

"I guess so," she answered. I asked her if anything was especially difficult. She thought about it. "Not really. I'm just not doing as well in AP Chemistry like my parents say."

Because it took me some time to understand what Diane meant by her responses, to determine what if anything she needed help with, I saw her again a week later. Ultimately, I came to the conclusion that Diane was very anxious to please her parents and to be a good kid, but she really didn't need tutoring in anything. It was her parents who needed tutoring. They needed to hear from someone professional that they should relax and appreciate how good a student they had in the family, even if she got one B.

Diane's case exemplifies when parents should definitely not tutor their child. This does not mean all parents who drive their children to learn and push them to be tutored are in the wrong. In another, similar case, I found that the child was really much more capable than he had been performing. It's just that his parents were pressuring him so often that he simply shut down rather than apply himself. Once tutoring helped him reestablish a connection to his work that was all his own, independent of his parents, he flourished. In short, you cannot generalize. Each case is different.

Also, and most important, Diane didn't want to be tutored. Any short-term gains would have come at the long-term cost of undermining her sense that she could learn well enough on her own.

My advice here is not some simplistic plea to avoid competition at all costs. Competition is not all bad. If the student is eager in some healthy way to correct or even deepen her understanding of a subject or skill, the proper tutoring can work well. There is nothing wrong with enrichment. And yet tutoring should not be driven by purely competitive motives, which usually come from an anxious parent.

In sum, tutoring shouldn't divert students' focus from their interests and strengths to what their parents want them to be. And it shouldn't contribute to a culture that insists students should worry about their grades and which college they go to at the expense of what they think. Tutoring should not be an instrument for alienating students from the ongoing process of understanding what inspires them or where their curiosities lie. The costs of this undesirable kind of tutoring would be to distance students from developing as young people and to contribute to the worst kinds of social pressure.

Students Whose Parents Want Them to Perform Flawlessly on the PSAT, SAT, or ACT

Jason, a junior in high school, had already taken the SAT twice and upped his scores considerably. Now his parents had heard that some tutors all but guaranteed they could raise students' SAT scores substantially. Jason's father believed that would make Jason's scores pretty near perfect. "We want our son to have this opportunity," the father declared. "And we're willing to pay for it."

Jason had worked hard and effectively in school, achieving very good but not superior grades. His SAT test scores were quite good. But even more to the point, they were in line with the kind of academic achievement he showed in school. His parents nonetheless insisted that his SAT scores were not good enough. They needed to be closer to 800. "Jason needs outstanding SAT scores to make him stand out," his father commented. "If your help works, it will put him over the top."

Clearly, Jason had come around to believing they were right. He was only too happy to have his parents find him this magical help. "Look," he told me privately, "I need better scores to get into where I want to go. I have to go to one of those schools. I won't be happy anyplace else. The whole problem is my SAT scores."

"What problem," I thought? In spite of Jason's declaration, I told his parents that tutoring him for the SATs was not a good idea.

"All right," the father said. "Thanks for your advice. But we're just going to go elsewhere."

Jason's parents refused to be comfortable with their son's development and his performance. Neither was Jason. If he were tutored further, it would have effectively continued to give the boy the message that the most important matters for his education were his score on this test and his matriculation at an elite college. All other colleges would simply be a disappointment and somehow wrong for him.

Tutoring Jason would have contributed once again to the hyper-competitive instincts of these parents. But there was an added, equally problematic twist: it would have implied to their son that when his performance wasn't immediately flawless, there was something wrong. There shouldn't be any sign of struggle as he learned. There was no need for patience. Never mind that some students blossom in college rather than in high school.

I'm sure Jason's parents found someone else who promised to help. There are undoubtedly tutors or tutoring companies who are only too glad to take advantage of overstressed parents. But I didn't think it was a good idea.

Rachel's situation was another matter. She was an exceptional student, entering her junior year of high school, but she had a history of poor test taking. Now her parents had contacted me because they didn't want their daughter's options for college affected by her difficulty at taking timed tests.

"She's a wonderful student," Rachel's mother explained, "bright, inquisitive, happy. But when you put her under pressure, something happens. She freaks out. She's at an excellent but loosey-goosey school. They give her plenty of time on tests and take the pressure away. So she does well. But it's always different when she has time constraints. It's going to be different when she takes the SAT."

"They're right," Rachel added. "I don't do well on tests. I want to get some help, but I'm not sure it will do anything."

"If there isn't anything that can be done, that's fine," Rachel's mother said. "We'll accept that as it is. But let's see if a little help works."

I agreed to tutor Rachel.

Unlike Jason's parents, Rachel's parents were not driven by competition or unrealistic expectations. They simply wanted to help their daughter overcome a difficulty and realize her potential. That was clear enough, because they were willing to accept the results if tutoring didn't help. Their attitude was altogether healthy, as was that of their daughter.

Rachel needed tutoring to overcome a specific problem caused by her lack of test-taking strategy and some accompanying anxiety. These made her knowledge and talents disappear when test time rolled around. She didn't need help scoring perfectly on the SAT; she needed help learning how to take tests so that she remained composed and focused.

The motivation of parents is critical to deciding who should be tutored. So is whether tutoring contributes to the student's ability and confidence in meeting academic challenges independently. Jason would have been undermined. Rachel was definitely helped.

Students Who Do Well in One Subject but Not Another

John, a freshman in high school, had an explanation for his current problems. "I've always been good at writing," he declared. "It's just this teacher. I don't like her, and she's a really hard grader, too. She's unfair."

John was doing just fine in his other subjects, but his work in English had declined over the course of two months, and with it had gone his pleasure in reading and writing. His parents were concerned. His father, a software salesman, stated tersely, "He should do better. We expect better from him." His mother, a nurse, said vaguely,

"Something is wrong." "Not really," John insisted. "It's the teacher. Watch what happens next year."

At first glance, I could not tell whether tutoring was the answer for John.

There were several possibilities to choose from:

- A consulting tutor to interview him and his parents and meet the precise need he had in English class.

- A counselor rather than a tutor to help him adjust to school. John might simply have channeled the difficulty of being a freshman in high school into his behavior or performance in English class.

- A counselor rather than a tutor to help him adjust to a pushy parent or some as yet unclear family dynamic. John's father might have placed special demands on him, hovering like a helicopter over his performance until John reacted poorly out of stress.

- Neither a counselor nor a tutor. In spite of what his parents and John reported, he might have overestimated his abilities in English or have been impatient for the pace of his development. He might simply have needed to pay attention, work hard, and trust that in the end he would improve.

It took two sessions of careful interviewing before I could pin down that he needed a swift, surgical kind of tutoring, which enabled him to adjust to the unique style of his teacher—*to learn how to learn* from her. He had reacted poorly to his teacher's comments because they were so severe in tone. But those comments were also really insightful and exactly right in their assessments of John's work. Properly understood, her comments could help him improve. After a short amount of tutoring, John began to appreciate her and did better in her class.

Students Who Have Been Diagnosed with ADHD and Urged to Medicate

Everyone adored William, a seventh grader newly admitted to an elite prep school on a nearly total scholarship. Charming, imaginative, and bright, William was instantly popular with students and teachers. But as school progressed during his first fall, William's energy became a concern in two of his classes. Teachers reported that although he was always respectful, William was just a little louder than most of the kids and occasionally at the center of some good-natured fun that interrupted the lesson. Interruptions were ordinary enough in seventh grade, the teachers reported, but William seemed to be part of the fun all of the time.

At the suggestion of the school, William went for a professional evaluation. In fact, the school had gotten the foundation providing William with a scholarship to pay for it. The psychologist diagnosed William with mild attention deficit hyperactivity disorder and offered a number of suggestions for treating him, including placing William on medication.

School officials told William's parents that medication made sense. Legally, they couldn't say that he had to be on medication. But medication really makes a difference in many cases, the school told the parents.

William's parents came to me. They were uncomfortable with putting their son on drugs.

"He's such a good kid," his father said. "Isn't he just being a boy?"

His mother asked, "Can't some kind of tutoring help him instead?"

William was clearly worried and confused. "I didn't know I was doing anything wrong," he said. "I really don't want to get kicked out of this school."

I referred William to a counselor. A counselor or therapist was better equipped because the issues involved appeared to be totally behavioral. Tutoring can affect behavioral issues, but tutoring is more typically the solution when the problematic behavior is the result of some academic issue—for example, if William's hyperactivity was the indirect result of his inability to write an essay. A counselor is more appropriate when the primary source of the difficulty is emotional or behavioral.

I later had contact with William's counselor and learned that William's so-called hyperactivity had two sources. One source was the excitement of being at a new school. The second source was cultural. He'd been at an inner-city school, where the classrooms were simply more raucous. Now he was in a much more restrained environment. To fit in, he needed to learn how to behave differently—at least in those classrooms where his teachers had shown their disapproval. He needed to learn how to "read" his teachers and the classroom environment better. The school assumed that William's past school environment was like its own, and it insisted that its environment remain a little more "buttoned up," no matter what his background was. With personal adjustment and more patience on all sides, William calmed down and flourished. Whatever attention problems he may have had seemed to go away.

William was a potential victim of a cultural tendency to overdiagnose ADHD. He came close to being tranquilized for the sake of creating a more homogeneous, quieter classroom environment.

Parents shouldn't generalize from William's story, however. In some cases of ADHD, medication may be necessary, and tutoring may be an essential companion to treatment. A pediatrician and a psychologist strongly recommended to parents that their ADHD-diagnosed son, Michael, be given Ritalin. But the parents had resisted for years until his school reported that their son was so distracted he could rarely focus on lessons. Michael spent most classroom time fidgeting, getting in and out of his seat, and staring out the window. The school counselor said that the boy had reached the point where he was "simply not available for learning." The parents finally agreed. The medication worked. The student gained newfound abilities to concentrate.

But the medication wasn't a magic pill. Even though it helped the student concentrate, he hadn't developed many of the necessary skills and study habits for learning. In this case, therefore, tutoring was also necessary to provide and improve Michael's academic skills.

As with other types of students, decisions on whether to tutor students diagnosed with ADHD are case by case. There is no single answer for all children. There is no one-size-fits-all solution.

Students Who Have Poor Study Habits

The same principle holds true for students with poor study habits. Some would benefit from tutoring. Some would not. Here are three cases that get at the most common issues parents face in making that decision.

Case Number One: Peter

Peter was seventeen years old and nearly a straight-A student, but as his junior year progressed, he procrastinated with increasing frequency, starting and completing assignments at the last minute. His grades were still excellent. Yet as the homework mounted, he continued to delay working until the last minute. By the middle of the school year, there was at least one night per week when he was barely sleeping. If this kept up, by the time Peter went to college, the workload would be impossible.

The case for tutoring Peter in work habits seemed clear enough. Or did it? I wondered if this was some kind of anxiety brought on by the pressures of applying to college. I wondered if his parents were driving him to distraction.

In fact, there turned out to be a clear, immediate cause for his current study habits: Facebook. He would shut the door to his room to study, turn on the computer, and four or five hours later realize he still had assignments to do.

"Hello, my name is Peter and I am a Facebook addict," he told me privately. "Don't tell them," he added, meaning his parents. "They'll go nuts."

Facebook, Instant Messaging (IM), You Tube, iTunes, and whatever Internet community comes next—these technologies have become a vital part of adolescent experience. And they don't necessarily signal a problem. One adolescent girl's tendencies to IM enriched her studying; another frittered her time away on gossip. Each case is different.

The same goes for video games. In one case I know, video games were an important but moderately used form of recreation that did not interfere with the student's ability to focus. He studied well and needed no tutoring. In another case, video games were an utter waste of time for the student and became solely a way in which he avoided learning how to develop his intellectual abilities and study habits. (Some studies report that excessive use of video games and television can decrease a student's ability to concentrate.)

These variations must be considered as you evaluate the unique needs of your child.

I understood that what mattered for Peter was how his study habits were influenced by Facebook and its Internet relatives, from iTunes to IM. Peter had exceptional abilities to concentrate on his work when he got down to it. In the end, he needed a modest, precise kind of help with time management, organization, and academic tutoring. Once this tutoring began, Peter certainly reduced his time on Facebook, but he continued to spend a considerable amount of energy using it. He just parceled out his time more effectively.

Case Number Two: Albert

Albert, a seventh grader, was a fascinating kind of mobile learner; that is, he actually learned a lot while he moved around rapidly.

"I got to be on the move," he declared. When I met him, he was perfectly happy to talk about his work, but after a full day of school, he just didn't want to stay seated. "I can do it," he told me, "but I'd much rather be doing this." He got up and paced the room, checking out books, leaning against a file cabinet, seating himself in another chair, and then popping up.

"Albert!" his mother said, raising her voice.

"It's OK," I replied.

"No," his mother said. "How's he ever going to get through high school this way?"

Albert was a pretty good student, with no signs that he had special difficulties in any subject. His school occasionally sent home reports that he'd been disruptive, but he was at a strict school. Almost all of the boys received these occasional reprimands. "We consider them honor points," Albert told me.

"Well, we don't," Albert's mother said.

Albert sighed loudly and looked at the ceiling, appealing to God.

Albert's mother asked, "Can you help us?"

I said that I would see if Albert needed help after spending more time with him. For two more sessions, I worked with him. Each time, he bounced around the room like a pinball, all the while focusing on the work he needed to do: studying for a history test, memorizing a poem, and even completing a math assignment (for which he landed long enough to scratch out calculations and show his work).

I ended my tutoring of Albert. I told the parents that they should simply give Albert time. If his style got in the way of his learning or made him consistently disruptive in class, then they should help him make changes. Right now, he was simply doing what he needed to do, and it seemed to be working.

When it came to study habits, Albert's parents imagined a quiet boy, leaning over his desk for hours on end. But Albert's idea of studying was more like a workout, and the great thing was that it worked out.

Albert's style may well be more common among boys than girls, which doesn't mean boys are inherently more restless or kinetic than girls. It means that more boys may be exhibiting this behavior at present, and they may be more scrutinized or judged for habits that don't necessarily cause a problem.

The last decade has shown a great deal of worry about "boy's restlessness" and assorted other behaviors that are identified as signs of maladjustment. That is what had Albert's mother so concerned. But Albert isn't an abstract, general phenomenon. He's an individual boy in need of individual assessment. Whether or not to tutor shouldn't be determined by general worry but by the specific circumstances of the case. Albert was all right.

Case Number Three: Bill

Bill, a sophomore in high school, was a mystery to both his teachers and his parents. "We think he's pretty smart," his father, a chiropractor, said wryly, "but whatever smarts he has are buried somewhere in his room." He asked that I come to their home so he could show me. Bill's room was impressive. One wall was covered with single pages taken from comic books—ranging from superheroes out of Marvel Comics to Japanese Manga. The closet on the wall next to it was forced open by a virtual landslide of tennis shoes, boots, roller blades, and soccer cleats on top of a heap that included shirts and blue jeans. A desk at the far corner was covered in piles of books of various heights that served as pedestals for action figurines. A book bag hung from the back of a desk chair. More precisely, the book bag hung on top of many layers of clothing, beneath which one could imagine there was the back of a chair.

On closer inspection of Bill's book bag, one could see that it contained a rat's nest of papers—returned assignments, handouts, and notes from various classes in no particular order. It also contained two notebooks filled with expertly executed line drawings of characters that Bill had apparently invented and drafts of text for complete comics, with the dates of their composition clearly noted.

Was all of this an outward sign of inward tumult? Bill had been having problems in a number of classes for nearly the entire school year. He turned in assignments late or in somewhat illegible form. He showed astonishing perception and ability in some parts of tests but gave incomplete answers in other parts.

Asked to summarize how he went about preparing for tests, Bill replied, "Same as for essays. I think about it, and then I just do it." He paused for a moment and then added, "I know there's more I can put on tests. I just draw a blank. It happens with essays, too. I forget that I had more to say until after I've turned them in."

Bill may be representative of a disorganized student, but his case shows that one must be careful in deciding whether or not to tutor. On the one hand, he clearly approached schoolwork in a pell-mell manner and was uncertain as to how he should organize his books and book bag. He was equally uncertain how to collect his thoughts on an essay or test in such a way that he could access and develop them easily. On the other hand, his work with comic books showed he had an extraordinary capacity for focus and organization. In classes, his thoughts and understanding were obscured to him beneath his messy style of learning. In his work at comics, he was masterly. Bill wanted to change, so he needed tutoring to help him effect a kind of translation: to use the organizational abilities he displayed with comics in other areas of study. He was able to do better in school with some tutoring.

Case by case, the decision to tutor should focus on determining whether or not the student's habits are impeding his or her ability to develop.

Students Who Have Been Diagnosed with an Autism Spectrum Disorder

To be complete, any discussion of whether or not to tutor these days must acknowledge what many parents face when they have children diagnosed as autistic. They too must decide whether a tutor helps or hinders their child, although the tutor they seek has highly specialized training. Imagine a three-year-old girl—we'll call her Cindy—who has been diagnosed with Pervasive Developmental Disorder Not Otherwise Specified (PDDNOS), because she has shown impairment in her social interactions and in her ability to use language. She doesn't smile or otherwise respond when an adult calls her name. She doesn't show much interest in watching or joining other children as they play. If adults point in a direction, she rarely follows the direction of their fingers or looks up to their faces to see what they might mean.

In recent years, treatment of autism has advanced to the point where many experts would assert that Cindy has a good chance of overcoming her disorder if she receives the right kind of intervention at an early age. As Cindy enters preschool, the school district insists that she be placed in a special program for children with autism. They say she can't be mainstreamed.

Cindy's parents object to this. If she is going to get better, they want her among all different kinds of children, where she can learn to communicate. They want her in the regular classroom, and they want the school district to provide an aide to work with her each week. After a lot of struggle, the school district relents and places her in the regular preschool classroom.

But as is often the case, the school supplies an aide who is not trained to provide the right kind of help. This aide simply follows Cindy around the class, keeping her quiet or distracted. The parents want the school to hire a more highly trained and credentialed professional to help Cindy with socialization and communication.

For this population of children, with whom I am certainly not trained to work, I wouldn't presume to offer a definitive opinion but only to acknowledge the difficult choices parents make as they try to balance giving their children what they need to develop without stigmatizing them. Again, there is no one, easy answer, and each special situation deserves its own custom solution, depending on the child, the school, the financial resources, and the professionals available.

Learning How to Learn: The Importance of Intellectual Independence

There is a fundamental reason to tutor that underlies all the individual assessments that parents should make. Students need a tutor when they need help gaining a kind of *intellectual independence*.

Intellectual independence does not mean that a student will suddenly learn all by himself or herself, in isolation from others. Rather, it's the ability to learn in the classroom, in the school more generally, and even outside of the school, if that is where the student's interests and talents lie. Students who have this kind of independence still need to go to the teacher for help on occasion, but they flourish while being repeatedly challenged in and out of their classrooms.

Learning by its very nature challenges students. As much as school instructs in subjects, from art to math, it teaches students how to develop their capacities to meet challenges, to solve problems, and to be comfortable with intellectual difficulty.

And yet there are students who are stuck. They have exhausted the resources of the school, from teachers to peers to resident learning specialists, and they continue to struggle unsuccessfully. They may have difficulties that the schools are simply ill equipped to address. They may need tutoring because they don't respond well to the style or the demands of the individual school. They may have trouble with the instructional style of a particular teacher. And on occasion, they may have a teacher who is inadequate or dysfunctional. In most cases, however, the student's need for tutoring has nothing to do with the quality of the teacher and everything to do with the student's becoming confident and independent at learning.

This confidence can be an elusive thing, part of the on-again, off-again state of puberty or adolescence, where at one moment the student is childlike and in need and at the next moment adultlike and scorning assistance. Students need tutoring when this confidence consistently escapes them and threatens their ability to develop, both in school and out of school.

At each turn, the answer to the question "Does my child need tutoring?" depends on the specifics of the case. Parents need to evaluate their child to see what exactly are their reasons and their child's reasons for considering tutoring. Tutoring shouldn't indulge the competitive instincts of parents. It also shouldn't exploit parents' anxieties about the future of their child to make a buck.

Instead it should provide help in achieving the goal of intellectual independence. In the long run, only that kind of independence can help a child's individual personality and character thrive. In tutoring, the best way to achieve this goal is to help students learn how they as individuals learn, so they can adapt their habits as need be. *Learning to learn* is the essential approach to tutoring that this book advocates—a comprehensive, transformative approach to tutoring that the next chapter describes.

CHAPTER ONE

Finding the Right Tutor for Your Child

You've decided your child needs tutoring. Now, like so many parents, you wonder how to go about choosing the right tutor for your child.

The Introduction addressed the issue of who needs to be tutored, the answer to which was a version of "It depends." Not every student with driven parents should be tutored nor should every child with apparently poor study habits. Yet some students are stuck and need help.

Once you've decided that your child needs tutoring, how do you select a tutor? That question typically includes three concerns:

- *What underlying approach should the tutor take?* I know my child needs help on his study skills or on a particular subject, but how should the tutor approach the subject?
- *What does good tutoring look like?* I know this tutor comes highly recommended, but how do I judge whether he or she is good for the unique needs of my child?
- *What qualifications should the tutor of my child have?* I know this tutor has an impressive education, but is

23

that the most important factor? What else should I be looking for?

What Underlying Approach Should a Tutor Take?

The answer to this question takes us to the heart of this book. It advocates for an ambitious style of tutoring that will benefit your child the most. The Introduction ended by describing a goal of tutoring: not simply teaching a skill or increased competency in subject matter but also helping a child achieve *intellectual independence*.

Intellectual independence refers to the ability of your children to face the necessary challenges of learning on their own, drawing on the resources of their schools. It also includes your children's belief that they can overcome learning challenges.

And so this goal includes not only your child's increased ability but also his improved outlook toward learning—not panic or pessimism but confidence and determination. Tutors should work themselves out of a job, returning the student to the normal struggles of being in school.

The benefits of tutoring in this way work for students at every level, and they go far beyond your children's school years. That's why the *independence* to which this term refers is distinctly *intellectual* rather than simply academic. Learning doesn't stop with the end of formal education. Adults, too, face such challenges. The absence of the ability to meet learning challenges can cripple development, but its presence can go a long way toward enabling someone to advance her life.

Parents should therefore select tutors who teach more than skills or subject matter. Tutors should also be able to develop intellectual independence within the students with whom they work. The focus of tutoring is then not simply enrichment but also *learning to learn*.

Learning Intellectual Independence

Let's look at the story of Carter to illustrate this approach. It doesn't matter what kind of student Carter is—whether strong or average in ability. It matters how he was helped.

When I first met Carter, three months into his freshman year of high school, he claimed that he was more frustrated with his parents than he was with his progress. They didn't understand, he told me. Middle school was over; high school was different. He was working as hard as he could.

Carter had attended a nurturing but weak middle school. He had been a good student there. His parents, a men's clothing salesman and a florist, were proud of him. Between middle school and high school, the family moved. He enrolled at a demanding high school, where everything was different for him.

He'd begun the year enthusiastic and confident, reporting to his parents how much he liked the classes and the students. That changed when he received a C-minus on his first substantial evaluation, an in-class essay on *The Odyssey*, by Homer. Carter was disappointed—"hurt and shocked," his mother reported. He reassured himself and his parents by stating that everyone in the class had done poorly.

In the next month, Carter continued to struggle. He scored a C-minus on a history test, received a mediocre grade on a lab report, and wrote another C-minus essay for English. His parents grew increasingly concerned and began to press him: Was he spending a lot of time on the phone or on the computer with friends? As a precaution, they restricted his use of the Internet and limited his television watching. The new restrictions had little effect on Carter's performance. His parents contacted me.

Carter was willing to accept my help, he said, but he did not truly believe anything would come of it. He told me that his teachers had pegged him as an average-to-below-average student, and there he would remain. "Just the same," I said, "Would you mind if I gave it a try?"

I looked over his classes, books, binders, and returned work. His binders were nearly empty of notes. His graded lab reports, tests, and essays were filled with comments urging him to analyze more deeply and to provide more detail. Watching me study his work, Carter casually revealed that other students met with teachers outside class, but he had rarely done so.

I pointed out the obvious: he had in effect refused his teachers' assistance by refusing to ask for it. "They don't help," he insisted. Clearly, he wasn't ready to pursue working individually with his teachers.

Within two weeks, Carter had another essay to prepare for English on *The Odyssey*. I watched him start out. He opened his book, looked over the small amount of notes he had taken in class, and reread two underlined passages in the epic. Then he began to write the first draft of his essay.

"I've read it all and listened in class," he explained, "so I just go."

I started to offer suggestions, but he found them distracting. He was once again not ready to hear them.

Later that week, he e-mailed me that the essay was tough going because he had forgotten a great idea. It had been in his head the week before.

At our next session, Carter showed me a copy of the essay he'd turned in. "It's not very good," he said.

"There's a reason for that," I said, "and if you're ready to listen, I think I can help you."

I told him that he hadn't developed any habits that helped him address writing or remember his thoughts on a book. In fact, he had no idea how he went about studying for any subject other than "I just go."

I established a process for reading and note taking that he began to use for all of his classes. I made him think rigorously about his argument and his organization as he prepared essays. I also insisted that he read his teachers' comments on all of his returned work. Once he began to follow this advice, it became apparent that Carter needed work in particular areas of analysis, especially inferential thinking. But he was a quick study.

In a short time, Carter's complaints about his abilities lessened. They didn't stop altogether. There were occasional lapses. Still, in the next few months, Carter focused on his difficulties. He began to seek out teachers, at first reluctantly but later willingly.

By the end of the next semester, Carter had made steady progress. His parents, too, saw that his confidence was back. He was learning intellectual independence. I ended my work with him.

One way to describe the origin of Carter's problems is that he had no clear sense of *how* to learn. He had never encountered genuine academic difficulty before he reached ninth grade. His experience in middle school did not help him, so he needed to learn that he was capable of overcoming challenges. His first reaction, however, had been despair and his second to commit himself to remaining in this state. He shut down. He preferred hopelessness to change when in fact he was at a new school that challenged him to develop his abilities to solve problems or to seek appropriate help.

For sixteen-year old Celia, a sophomore in high school with ADD, the problem was slightly different. She insisted that she knew how she learned. If she had an essay to write, she knew exactly what her ideas were. She wrote them down. She opened her notebook to show pages of notes that literally covered all white space on the pages, a sea of ink in which any attempt to focus her thinking quickly drowned.

When Celia went to write an essay, her ideas didn't come together, except as a list of seemingly disconnected thoughts. Sometimes she had a really good thesis statement, she said, but the teacher always told her it had nothing to do with the other ideas in her essay. It was totally frustrating. She worked so hard. Where was the reward for all that hard work?

Celia's unfiltered style of taking notes was the tip of the iceberg. Overall, she had a way of working that guaranteed there would be a disconnection between her particular and her general observations. The problem appeared in more than essays and reading, too. When she studied for tests in science, she slaved for hours. But general principles were lost amid a swarm of facts and details.

Celia knew something was wrong, but she was unable to see its source. As we examined how she learned, she was open to changing her habits. She learned to prioritize, to distinguish the more-important ideas from the less-important ones. Her notes began to serve as a filter for her experience of class and of reading. Her work gradually improved.

For Carter and Celia, their problems with writing were a symptom. The style with which they met learning challenges was its cause. They lacked a clear sense of how they went about their work and which of their habits stopped them from working more easily. Once a tutor taught them *how* they learned, they were ready to make changes. They developed intellectual independence.

Different Styles of Learning

Parents may recognize Carter and Celia's styles of learning. There are also many other styles of learning that can lead students to trouble. Here are a few more examples:

- A fifteen-year-old student's style was to wait until the last minute to do an assignment, prepare for a test, or write an essay, because the student believed that it led to better concentration and performance—and it was more exciting.

- A fourteen-year-old with ADHD raced through history readings and then despaired that she couldn't ever remember the details.

- A thirteen-year-old had his "own way of doing math," which didn't require showing any work. He was infuriated that he always made careless mistakes on tests.

- A sixteen-year-old had been told so often she was brilliant that she ripped up every draft of an essay unless it immediately met her expectations. Preparing papers was sheer torture for her.

Parents may look over this list, nod their heads, and declare each of these styles to be problems. But that's too general. Not every student who learns in these styles needs help, at least not immediately. The students I encountered did, however, because their habits had inhibited their ability to meet the challenges of their education. They were frustrated, angry, anxious, or despairing.

Once these students were shown how the styles they had adopted caused their problems, they were more open to changing their habits. And once they changed their habits, they were profoundly more available for learning. They were able to fix their problems and become independent of me rapidly. They developed intellectual independence.

Parents should therefore look for tutors who do more than teach their children geometry, explain chemical bonds, analyze *Jane Eyre,* or tease out the causes of the French Revolution. They should look for tutors who build their children's ability to learn independently by teaching them *how* they learn, reinforcing good habits, and replacing bad ones. Even as tutors focus on the necessary subjects and skills, they should teach the students about their own learning style.

Parents should expect tutors to make use of any resources available to determine what their child's learning style is. The list of potential resources is long. It includes parents, teachers, learning specialists, neuropsychologists, child psychiatrists, social workers, psychologists, school counselors, and anyone else who formally or informally has evaluated their child. A good tutor will be comprehensive and vigilant at gathering information on how the student learns. The more complete a sense of how the student learns, the better the tutor can work with the student.

What Does Good Tutoring Look Like?

It's one thing for tutors to declare that they want to make students independent and confident. It's quite another to achieve this goal for your individual child. Understandably, parents want to know how to detect if the tutor they select is succeeding. My work with Chloe is a good example of what parents should pay attention to.

Over the phone, Chloe's mother explained that Chloe, a thirteen-year-old eighth grader, was "very upset" for the second time in as many days. School overwhelmed Chloe, her mother reported, even though she was intelligent and capable. On any given evening when she sat down to study, she interrupted herself frequently with phone calls and instant messaging. Her mother believed that Chloe did that because she was frustrated and uncertain of how to work, especially in history and English. Could I help?

When I met Chloe and her mother, Chloe told me a different story. She was simply unhappy at her school. She worked steadily and without interruption each night, sometimes until eleven o'clock or midnight. Did she instant-message while she studied? Of course not. She pursed her lips and shot a glance at her mother. Did she make phone calls? Rarely, and only when it helped her work. The problem was, Chloe explained, she was unhappy. That's all. Then she started to cry.

This wasn't the time to point out to Chloe that her explanation of her problem made no sense. It also wasn't the moment to ask her if she was stretching the truth about her study habits. I handed her a tissue and asked to see her alone from then on.

During my next visit with Chloe, she did a spectacular job of avoiding work. She claimed that she had done it all. (This was clearly not the case.) She wanted to discuss the schools she preferred to attend rather than the one she was at. I told her that I'd do my best to help her go to the school of her choice. But she needed to be able to work better if she were to have a chance to attend that terrific school she so wanted.

My focus on her goal pleased her a great deal. Then I told her that if she wanted my help, she should always bring in all of her work, including recently returned work.

She glowered at me. She accused me of being just like her mother. I said, "Far from it. I'm here to help you get what you want if you want to be helped. But it's your choice. Otherwise, I can't help you." Slowly, Chloe began to reveal her work habits to me. First, she admitted that on rare occasions she used instant messaging. Next, she told me that at night, she sometimes talked with friends about something other than school. In time, she admitted she used instant messaging and the phone a lot. She studied for about an hour and a half per night rather than the four hours she had originally reported.

Then we began to look at why she had been avoiding her work. Each time she faced something that was difficult in English and history, she grew frustrated. She dismissed the work as irrelevant to her life. I appeared to sympathize with her but only briefly. Then I refocused her on the challenge.

It turned out that her problems began with reading itself. Unlike math, reading just wasn't "definite" enough, as she put it. She was uncomfortable with the ambiguity of reading a novel or understanding the variety of influences that determined a historical event. Faced with such uncertainty, she gave up. I taught her a way of gaining greater ease while reading. It involved providing her with a systemized approach to what she read. In history, it included making separate outlines of important historical events on the one hand and causes and influences on the other. Chloe then compared the causes-and-influences outline with the important-historical-events outline to evaluate the significance of an event—and then did it in the reverse. In English, it began with her outlining the plot; listing important speech, actions, and descriptions of characters; and eventually identifying themes. Each step made Chloe more comfortable with the ambiguities of reading by imposing organization on it.

Chloe began to complete reading assignments regularly, first with a tentative understanding of what she read and then with some confidence. That led to work on writing. By the middle of the next semester, she was turning in all of her work on time and had increasingly less worry about either history or English.

Along the way, her mother reported that Chloe had changed her mind. She liked her school a little more than she had thought. Maybe she didn't have to change schools after all.

Three Characteristics of Good Tutoring

Your child may be far different from Chloe. And yet her story identifies three characteristics of good tutoring that you should focus on as you evaluate which tutor will be effective with your child:

- The tutor gains the trust of the student, who increasingly reveals what the experience of learning is like, including what gets in the way.
- The student doesn't think of the tutor as either a parent or a teacher.
- The tutor helps the student by supplying specific habits and skills that ease the student's ability to adapt to the challenges of particular subjects or the pedagogical style of a particular teacher.

The Tutor Gains the Trust of Your Child

Tutoring won't do much good unless students believe it's worth telling the tutor how they are struggling. Students must feel comfortable disclosing as much as they can about their difficulties. If they don't, tutors won't have much to work with. Just as important, it may be a sign that your child has little faith that the tutoring will help or is simply not ready to be tutored.

Parents should therefore look for whether the tutor they select is building a rapport with their children. You must believe your children will reveal to the tutor all the relevant aspects of their school habits, including what work they do or fail to do, how they study, and any other details of their learning experience. Without this trust relationship, the core of a student's problems won't be addressed, and the student will be unlikely to make changes at the tutor's suggestion.

That trust isn't easy to achieve. A bright sixteen-year-old I worked with lied to me and to his parents for nearly two months until he was expelled from school for not doing his work. With that student, knowing how and when to talk to him was challenging, as it can be for many students. The tutor you should select must be able to speak the language of your child.

The personality and timing of the tutor can be important for establishing a connection with your child. For example, I had a timid thirteen-year-old student whom I managed to alienate by pushing her to work harder at exactly the wrong moment to make such a demand. After that, she withdrew. As much as I tried to convince her that I was a kinder, gentler person than she had thought, I'd blown it through my misperception of when to speak and what to say.

As parents evaluate a tutor, they should observe whether the rapport between the student and the tutor seems to be developing. You should look for signs that your child believes in the ability of the tutor and shows as much through words and actions, however gradually those signs occur.

The Tutor Is Neither Parent nor Teacher

To a young person, tutors can be those rarest of creatures: adults who don't punish them, bother them, order them around, or give them a grade. Tutors aren't going to take away their privileges or cramp their style. Tutors aren't going to jeopardize their futures with a C or D for the semester. On top of that, tutors aren't in their face every day at school or when they get home. Parents should select tutors who exploit this difference to the hilt.

A tutor often needs to avoid being directly associated with parents or teachers. They should forge a relationship with the student that is less antagonistic than it sometimes is with parents and less freighted than it can be with teachers.

For example, I worked with a fifteen-year-old who was challenged by ADHD. The student's progress at adjusting to it had been slowed as much by the volatile relationship she had with her mother as by anything else. They fought constantly. The mother's well-intentioned desire to be active in her daughter's education made matters worse. So the student responded by hiding her work from both of her parents. That way, her mother couldn't look it over.

In tutoring, I had to reassure the student repeatedly that I wouldn't share her work with her mother. The student also wanted assurances that I wasn't going to behave like her mother. She wanted my assistance but only if she asked for it. I couldn't be seen as insisting that I help. As the student grew to believe me, she progressed rapidly.

In this and many other cases, the very act of tutoring created a different relationship with an adult for the student, one where she could assess her work in relative tranquility.

Parents shouldn't expect the tutor to be an extension of themselves. The tutor's work, including the tutor's reports to parents about that work, shouldn't be something the student associates with the disciplining parents must do. The parent of one student with whom I worked had the habit of waiting until she and her son were in front of me to express her displeasure with his work. I had to encourage the mother to wait for a more private moment to scold her child.

Tutors should be distinctly more neutral in their response to a student (unless it involves some success). They shouldn't express much disappointment when a student fails to meet a goal or show impatience at the student's rate of progress if it is slow.

That does not mean that a tutor should baby students, treat them as victims of their difficulties, or patronize them. One thirteen-year-old student enjoyed working with me but consistently failed to complete the tasks that we had set for him to finish by the next meeting. I told him gently but firmly that I would have to cancel our meetings if he didn't make an honest effort to complete his work for each session. He changed his behavior very quickly.

Parents should also expect tutors to have a distinctly different relationship to their children than teachers do. Unlike teachers, tutors have the ability to observe a student alone for extended time and to provide sustained, personalized instruction. Teachers can provide intense, occasional scrutiny of individual students; but as I found while teaching college and high school, there is never enough time to work individually with each student on a regular basis. Teachers also know the importance of maintaining a kind of studied distance from students. They have to challenge the students and then give the students time to meet those challenges on their own.

Tutors provide some of that studied distance, but they offer considerably more close scrutiny and advice. Without spoon-feeding or excessive hand-holding, they observe and comment on the student's thinking and habits.

Gabe, a sixteen-year-old, Spanish-speaking boy with whom I worked, for example, was tentative and withdrawn in English. He was terrified of his teacher because the teacher was demanding and a hard grader. This was no fault of the teacher, who was known to be an excellent instructor.

There was no doubt that English was a tough subject for Gabe. He improved because we focused on interpreting his teacher's comments and helping Gabe to follow them. In the tutoring sessions, I challenged him as much as his teacher wanted him challenged. But Gabe temporarily needed the circumstances that tutoring provided. In tutoring sessions, he learned to concentrate on his teacher's instructions without feeling intimidated or judged by the threat of grades. Tutoring also provided him with concrete habits that he could rely on for improving his ability to analyze and to write. Eventually, he gained from his English class and even enjoyed it sometimes, even if he wasn't a great student.

The Tutor Helps Your Child Adjust to School

Let's look at Chloe and Carter again. As she was tutored, Chloe rethought her desire to change schools. During tutoring, Carter learned to make use of the resources at his school. Both changed their relationship to school through tutoring. They learned to handle the workload of school, seek out teachers for help, and meet their particular challenges through what tutoring provided. In the Introduction, I described John, who needed a brief, precise form of tutoring to adapt to the style of teaching in one class. As all of these cases demonstrate, part of learning is adapting to the pedagogical style of the teachers and the school. It is part of the goal of intellectual independence.

So parents should expect tutors to avoid making judgments of the school or the teachers in front of the student. In fact, tutors should strive to make students able
to learn in spite of their difficulties with individual teachers. Although the student may complain about particular
teachers, the tutor should focus on helping the student
analyze what the teacher requires and the challenges of
the teacher's class. Consider Gabe once more. He learned
how to listen and how "to read" his English teacher as
part of the process of tutoring.

A focus on helping the student adapt to the teacher
is also prudent. It's likely that the tutor doesn't know the
teacher or has at best only partial knowledge of what is
going on in the class. Instead, the tutor knows only the student's experience. It is also possible that a student's attitude
toward a teacher or a school can change substantially. Chloe
had just this kind of wholesale change in her attitude.

Parents should expect the tutor to help a student adjust
to a school, because the tutor's authority with a student
should in most cases be temporary. It shouldn't override
the central importance of the school in your child's education. Although tutoring is distinct and significant, it is not
a substitute for the classroom. The tutor's work with a student is reactive. It responds to the school, the subject, and
the teacher rather than replaces them. The tutor shouldn't
make the student dependent on the tutor for instruction;
tutors should return students to the teacher and classroom
as soon as possible.

What Qualifications Should a Tutor Have?

Across the nation, tutoring centers have been set up in
suburbs and on city streets. Well-funded chains advertise that they have just the test to ferret out the problems

your child is having. They promise to diagnose your child by using a standardized test, teach him or her the proper study skills, and improve your child's test scores and grades. The solutions these centers provide for your children, however, depend less on your child's unique style than on your child's general type.

Certainly, there are similarities between some students and study techniques that work with many students. But for most students with difficulties, to make changes in how they learn requires distinctly more individualized attention. If you look back on the teachers who most affected you, those who changed how you thought and learned, you'll see that they connected to you in some profound way. They were able to explain a subject in a way that stayed with you for years. It is likely that you remember that teacher because you appreciated some deeply personal connection with the teacher's style.

The qualifications of a tutor that you should focus on are those intangibles that have been identified in earlier sections of this chapter:

- The ability to teach students how they learn and thereby transform their ability to meet challenges
- The ability to build trust with students
- The commitment to making students independent

Parents will know what these look like in a tutor when they see it in practice.

There are also other necessary if more obvious qualifications. Expertise matters if a tutor is going to meet the unique needs of your child. Parents should seek someone who is capable of assessing the student's difficulties and instructing in the exact skills or subjects where the student's difficulties lie.

You wouldn't select someone without the appropriate experience to tutor reading to a dyslexic or tutor organization to someone with executive-functioning problems (*executive functioning* refers to the ability to manage the many tasks of life, including the completion of assignments and the necessary studying for tests and quizzes at school). You wouldn't expect someone without knowledge of Dostoyevsky or Tolstoy to tutor in Russian literature.

Training in the relevant subject matter or skill is important; and yet it isn't enough to say, "The more education, the better the instructor." A college student I know struggled in his elementary chemistry course because of the inability of his instructor, a renowned physical chemist, to teach at such a basic level.

To some extent, the capacity to teach the fundamentals of chemistry, physics, mathematics, English, or history develops in an instructor through experience. If I were to generalize, I'd prefer a seasoned tutor to a recently graduated college student. But these are simply generalizations. The point is for parents to evaluate the expertise of tutors to ensure that they are both educated in the subject area *and* able to convey what they know in a style that fits your child.

Parents should also select a tutor with experience working with the age and grade level of the student. At the urging of a testing neuropsychologist, I briefly took on an eight-year-old student in elementary school until I realized I simply didn't know how to instruct someone that young.

In sum, parents should select a tutor who can teach their children how they learn, and who can use that knowledge to create new styles of learning for them. When students understand *how they learn*, they become better able to adjust to the challenges of their education.

They find it easier to break destructive habits and to form new, constructive ones. Building on the unique learning style of each student, the tutors that parents select should provide more than occasional help with homework. They should help change students into increasingly confident and effective learners.

The tutor doesn't do this alone, however. Parents know their children, and they should use that knowledge first to select a tutor who makes that happen and, second, to create the circumstances that will make the tutoring process successful. Those circumstances are the subject of the next chapter.

CHAPTER TWO

Expectations and the Tutoring Process

Even if tutors establish rapport with your children and work hard to develop their intellectual independence, the process of tutoring can still be undermined unless parents and children have realistic and constructive expectations for the outcome of tutoring. This chapter addresses those expectations and describes how parents, students, and tutors should frame the tutoring experience.

In my first year as a tutor, I worked with a fifteen-year-old student named Howard. His father, a high-level executive at a bank, declared clearly what he expected to happen as I tutored Howard.

"We want you to focus specifically on reading comprehension in English and essay writing," he said. "His grades matter now that he is in high school. His English grade should be higher. How long will this take?"

"I don't know," I told him. "I need to see what his difficulties are. Tutoring doesn't always lead to a rapid change in grades."

He frowned but said nothing. Then he mentioned in passing that one person—he didn't identify whom—blamed Howard's difficulties in English on organizational problems.

That person was right. Howard planned little about his work in English. Whether it was getting his reading done or writing an essay, he was forever playing catch-up. When he sat down to write, his notes were in such chaotic form—scribbled on loose paper; scattered as marginalia in his copy of the book; and jotted down randomly amid math notes, science notes, and history notes—that it took nearly as much time to collect and make sense of them as to write a draft. Whatever ability he had to reflect on a topic was undermined by his disorganized style. Lots of ideas came to him, tumbling out of him pell-mell. So far, he had simply left them in that chaotic state, making it difficult for him to assemble them and ultimately to concentrate on any of them.

A Cautionary Tale

I told Howard we needed to start with his overall organization skills, from planning when he'd get the work done to how he approached specific reading and writing assignments.

Howard was puzzled by my advice. "But if I have an assignment due, how am I going to get a decent grade on it? I'll be spending all this time working on organization? I'm a freshman in high school," Howard said. "I need my grades to get better fast—for college."

"We'll work on the individual assignments," I said, "but you need to put yourself in a position to focus well on each of them."

I wrote out specific recommendations for him to use in order to organize his work. I showed him how to break down assignments into manageable daily tasks that he should begin well in advance of due dates. I also advised him to collect his notes only in a single notebook or in the margins of what he read. I assured him again that we would focus on individual reading and writing assignments.

Howard's father had asked for frequent reports on our work. When I described my initial approach to him, he wasn't pleased. "I'm sure your intentions are good," he said, "but Howard needs to get better grades on individual assignments first. He needs to see a little success. Then you can address the organization issue. So please stop it with the organizational part of your focus and stick to whatever immediate reading and writing assignment he has."

A Compromise That Fails

Against my intuitions, I agreed to do what Howard's father wanted on a temporary basis and see how it worked out. The next Monday, Howard informed me that he had an essay due on the following day but that he hadn't started it yet. The essay required at least one long evening of work if Howard was going to do simply an adequate job. He had one evening left and a lot of other homework besides English to do that night. The best I could do in the circumstances was a kind of triage. On Monday evening, he spent fewer than two hours knocking out a superficial and inadequate English paper, then went on to assignments for his other classes, which kept him up until nearly one in the morning. His grade on that English paper was a C. He was embarrassed. His father was clearly angry with him. I hoped this proved that another approach was necessary, but the father made no mention of what I'd originally recommended.

"He can't keep getting these kinds of results," his father stated flatly to me.

I urged Howard to give me advance notice of essay assignments from here on. I told him that he couldn't really improve his reading and writing if he was constantly rushing to complete work. And yet he followed the same habits for the next six weeks.

During those weeks, I made limited progress toward improving his reading ability. I helped a small amount with his writing, most of it the result of using his graded essays to instruct him on how he might have written them differently. But my efforts were not effective because we spent most of the time addressing assignments that were overdue or about to be due.

After several weeks, Howard's father surveyed the results and stated flatly to me, "I'm not seeing improvements from your work with him. His grades aren't better. I'm afraid this isn't working out."

I was dismissed, and Howard never improved his organizational skills or his grades.

What Went Wrong

There are many ways to think about what went wrong in Howard's case. Mistakes were made—some of them by Howard's father, some by Howard, and some by me. Howard's father expected the work to be immediately and relentlessly focused on specific reading and writing assignments. Meanwhile, I let Howard's father determine how I should tutor his son.

Underlying all of the mistakes was the assumption that tutoring should result in a swift improvement in grades. Any part of tutoring that didn't lead directly to better grades was a problem for Howard and his father. That expectation doomed Howard's tutoring from the start. It led him to resist important changes in his habits.

It led his father to devalue critical elements of how best to tutor his son, and it ultimately led to my dismissal.

Howard's grades might have improved more rapidly if his tutoring had been focused on the proper goal. Still more important, he would have been better able to read and to write well in the years to come—key ingredients in building his intellectual independence.

And yet Howard and his father felt a relentless pressure for Howard to get better grades. That pressure redirected a constructive approach to tutoring toward a primary focus on competition. Instead of placing the emphasis on Howard learning to learn as best as possible, the two of them wanted the emphasis to be on getting Howard the grades that would make him a candidate for the best colleges around.

Howard and his father are not alone in giving in to this pressure. I know well-intentioned parents who cannot stop themselves from rewriting their children's essays, including providing them with ideas and even crafting sentences if not entire paragraphs. I had a parent who was so focused on grades for her child that she wrote a paper for him (and was caught by the school). In each case, the expectation of getting better grades undermined the effort to make a student a more confident, independent learner. It sabotaged the process of tutoring.

Basic Assumptions and Expectations

An obsessive desire for higher grades isn't the only expectation that can throw off—or, for that matter, enhance—tutoring. Other important expectations appear in the strategic decisions that parents and students make about a host of important issues: the length of time your child needs to be tutored, the demands placed on your child for each tutoring session, and the amount and kind of support you believe the tutor should provide.

These decisions affect whether tutoring will increase a student's intellectual independence. They come out of expectations of what a student can and cannot do or of what effect tutoring should have. Consider these cases as typical:

- "My sixteen-year-old has some problems in history, but we don't want him to become dependent on a tutor. I think a short, intensive tutorial should solve the issue—no more than five weeks."

- "My fifteen-year-old needs your help, but if you put too much pressure on her to do work from one tutoring session to the next, she'll just shut down. Don't expect too much from one session to the next."

- "My fourteen-year-old has executive-functioning problems. It's almost impossible for him to meet all the deadlines for assignments, especially during crunch time. Tutoring sessions won't be enough. He and I both would like the tutor to supplement those weekly sessions with daily phone and e-mail contact to make sure he's staying on track."

- "Next week, my daughter has two essays and two mid-term exams. Would you stay for twice as long to help her get through all this work? Would you come an extra day, too?"

Both parents and students drive these kinds of requests. Whether they or their underlying expectations help your child develop intellectual independence depends on the individual circumstances. Let's look closer at each of these kinds of cases.

Setting Limits on How Long Your Child Needs to Be Tutored

"I'm a take-charge kind of person," Seth's mother declared, "but Seth has really got me at my wit's end." Seth was an eighth grader at a pretty good school, so far as she could tell, but he continued to perform below average in history.

"Here's what is happening," Seth's mother said. "At school, he's just not doing it, especially in history. At home, it's a different matter. Ask him about hip-hop, and he's encyclopedic. The most famous to the most obscure singers. You name it, he knows it. And on computer games, too, he's the best among his friends.

"Meanwhile, his history teacher thinks Seth can do better. I don't expect him to be a star student, but I won't let him be lazy."

She paused and then suddenly shifted directions. "Maybe he does need help. But here's my hesitation about tutoring: I don't want to see Seth get dependent on you. He's got to stand on his own two feet. He's not going to go all his life with somebody holding his hand."

I told her that I understood her concern but that the point was to make him independent.

"Well, I've thought of a solution to my worry." She held up her hand, with her fingers fully spread before me. "Five weeks," she said. "You've got five weeks with him. He's got five weeks with you. If there are improvements, then great. If there's no improvement, then he moves on without you."

"I don't know whether five weeks will produce results," I told her.

"We'll see. He knows he's got five weeks."

Seth wanted to be tutored, but he was a little exasperated by the circumstances. "So you're my boot camp instructor," he said. "Isn't boot camp about five weeks long?"

"I don't know," I told him. "Let's see if we can't ignore the time period and focus on what's making matters difficult."

I asked him if he knew what made history hard for him. He answered, "I don't know. In spite of what my mother says, I'm trying to do better."

Seth was indeed making a decent effort in history, but on the more demanding assignments, he was struggling. He had difficulty seeing the relationship between historical events and their underlying social and political circumstances, which his history course required. The rich soil of the Piedmont may have led him to understand the attraction of agriculture to colonial Virginia, but it didn't lead him to see the further connection to the development of slavery.

If I spelled out the connection for him, he appreciated the insight into history. "Now, I get it." He smiled thinly.

"We can work on this," I encouraged him.

He seemed to consider this seriously, but he didn't reply.

Each week, he greeted me by counting off the time we had together. "Welcome to week two," he announced at the beginning of our second week. "We're past halfway," he said seven days later, "It's been real."

Each week, I reminded Seth that he needed to practice historical analysis—to get used to conceptualizing and making associations. We used the readings of the course to exercise his ability. For each primary document he was assigned, I asked him to relate it to the events described in his general history book: Why were indentured servants such a force in Virginia? Why would they affect the relationships between the colonists and the Native Americans?

Seth dutifully replied to all of my questions, but he waited for me to push him to analyze. He rarely volunteered any understanding.

When the fifth week ended, I had no clear sense that he had made progress. His teacher reported only one notable change: Seth seemed a little more enthusiastic. He was participating more in class.

The real surprise came when Seth's mother announced that she had agreed to allow him to continue with tutoring. "He said he wants to do it," she explained, "and I gave it some thought. I'm not going to get in the way."

With the time constraint lifted, Seth changed almost immediately. He became a far more energetic student in tutoring. "Week six!" he announced when I arrived the following week. "Just kidding. No more counting." He concentrated more and tried to analyze without my prompting.

When I told him he seemed different, he shrugged his shoulders. "Boot camp is over. I feel free."

Seth began to improve. He understood what he needed to do, and he became both less frustrated and more patient with his progress. By the end of the semester, it was clear that he had gained confidence that he could do this work on his own.

The real obstacle to Seth's tutoring was the limit on time that Seth's mother had placed. She expected he would become dependent on tutoring. She also expected that an arbitrary time limit would make the process of tutoring work better.

Instead, it made Seth less productive. He was constantly looking over his shoulder, unenthusiastic, because he thought his mother was intruding. As soon as his mother removed the time limitation, he went from passive to active almost overnight. In Seth's case, the limit on time that his mother had imposed didn't help the process of tutoring. It deterred his ability to gain intellectual independence through tutoring.

Limiting Expectations from One Session to the Next

On the phone, Gloria's mother described her daughter as a frustrated student who in the face of persistent difficulties in several subjects gave up quickly. In ninth grade, Gloria had flunked English and would have flunked math if it hadn't been for an understanding teacher and a promise to do remedial work in summer school.

Gloria's mother and father appeared to be sensitive and loving parents. They knew Gloria needed help, and they declared themselves ready to be patient with her.

"We'll do all we can to help you with her," Gloria's mother said.

"But I think she doubts that anything can help her. She just has no confidence," her mother said. "You'll have to go slowly with her. She's much more fragile than it seems."

Gloria's mother was worried that her daughter would be overwhelmed with the work, as she was during ninth grade. They were even considering a less-demanding school, but they didn't want Gloria to be uprooted from her life with her friends.

"We don't expect her to keep up with all of the assignments all of the time. We just want you to help her see if she can do the work, even if she is getting C's or D's."

From Gloria's mother's description, I imagined that my first focus with Gloria would be helping her complete assignments on time with some degree of satisfaction. In this way, little by little, we'd build up a record of accomplishment for her.

When I met Gloria, she appeared tentative and a little shy. She sat uncomfortably at the edge of her chair. I asked her how she thought that I could help her.

"I don't know," she said. "I'm not a very good student. I'm not very good in math and English." She looked down, embarrassed, after she spoke.

"Do you want help?" I asked her.

"If it works," she said, "but I get frustrated," she warned me.

Gloria was going to receive extensive help in school for her math work, so we focused on English, beginning with her critical-reading abilities. Her class was assigned *All Quiet on the Western Front*. For each reading assignment, they had to prepare a page of notes. I asked Gloria if she thought she could get the reading done in advance of our next session. We could then focus on her note taking. She didn't think that would be a problem.

When we met again, Gloria announced that she had finished only half of the reading. "I tried," she said. "It was really long, and I got tired."

"That's fine," I said. We focused on taking notes on the first half of the reading. Slowly, I began to ask her about the plot and setting of what she had read.

She began with a general statement. "It's about a war, these guys who are in a war. They've just come back from where the fighting is." Shortly, with a few more questions, she managed to expand on the plot, identifying the time as World War I and the place as "somewhere in Europe."

Then I asked her about the characters. She said, "I don't really know. They're males. They don't like where they are. They don't like some other things, but I'm not sure what they don't like." She pursed her lips and looked out the window.

"Let's see if we can't find out a bit more from some of the passages in the book," I said.

By the end of the session, Gloria had slowly added to her understanding of the characters. At times, she had shaken her head and said, "I can't do this." But I'd persisted, and she had in the end described two main characters as young and shocked from what they had seen in battle. She could also see that they had been humiliated by the officer who trained them. She completed more than half a page of notes. This seemed to give her satisfaction.

Before Gloria left, I asked her why she thought she hadn't completed the reading. "I'm actually not sure," she said. "I thought I could do it, and then it started to take longer than I thought. Then my mother got worried I was doing too much, so I stopped."

Based on her answer, I told her that for next time, it was important that she try to finish the assigned reading entirely. "Just give it a little harder try and see how you do."

"All right," she said uncertainly.

Hours later, I received a call from her mother. She said that Gloria was upset. "You have to be careful you don't give her too much. I told her she didn't have to complete the reading before she saw you. She should just do what she could. Isn't that enough?"

By our next session, Gloria had finished about half the reading again. Her understanding of the reading was slightly better. On her own initiative, she identified plot elements and some details about the characters. She told me that she'd stopped halfway through "because my mother thought that was probably enough." I asked her again to do all the reading for next time.

After the session, I phoned her mother. I told her that Gloria might be able to do all the reading as I had asked.

"Why don't we let her try to make a full attempt this next time?"

"I don't know about this. She'll get upset again," her mother responded. "But I'll try not to say anything. It's just hard to watch your child get upset."

Gloria arrived at the next session with most of the reading done. A week later, she completed the full assigned reading. This was a small but important victory.

There was little doubt that Gloria had her difficulties in English, but tutoring helped her overcome some of them and gain confidence, once we removed the expectation that she was too fragile to meet reasonable demands—demands that were carefully adjusted to her abilities.

Gloria learned that she was more capable than she'd believed. She wasn't working under a cloud that she was too wounded or limited. That bolstered her confidence, which she directly related to the process of tutoring.

Gloria's mother had overestimated her daughter's fragility, which in turn had led her to adjust every expectation of Gloria's performance in school downward. Those reduced expectations had interfered with the process of tutoring. They had prevented Gloria from considering that tutoring might be a different environment for her than school or home, an environment where she might take risks and discover different ways to go at her work. The worries about her delicacy had delayed her discovery that through tutoring she could improve her reading and meet her workload.

Gloria's mother's reaction was understandable (even if it was unusual to find a parent with low expectations for her child). Gloria's mother had seen her daughter's distress at its fullest. She believed wholly that her daughter was fragile. Like any caring parent, she didn't want Gloria to be further damaged by an overwhelming workload. She tried to protect Gloria.

Once her mother supported my request that Gloria try to meet the goals we agreed to, Gloria changed. She *tried differently* than she had in the past. Her upset lessened as she worked. She began to improve.

More on Limiting Expectations

The expectation that students cannot complete an agreed-upon amount of work for each tutoring session has the potential to undermine the process of tutoring. It can persuade students that they are less able to gain from tutoring. It can convince them that they are less able to create new habits from tutoring and less able to become independent learners.

That expectation doesn't always come from the parents. I worked with a sixteen-year-old student who had been diagnosed with modest learning disabilities. From a young age, he had convinced his parents and a succession of tutors that he was far more disabled than he actually was. He used these lowered expectations to manipulate these tutors into coddling him and in some cases doing his work. The student managed to continue in this way through his sophomore year in high school when the roof caved in: he had not learned how to do math, to read, or to write on his own well enough to continue at his school.

In both Gloria's and this student's cases, expectations of how little the student could do prevented tutoring from advancing the intellectual independence of the student.

And yet the point made here shouldn't lead parents or tutors to create expectations that are too tough or insensitive for a student's abilities. Gloria's case doesn't mean that parents or students are wrong every time they expect less than a tutor requires from one session to the next.

For example, Lloyd, a fifteen-year-old, was all too eager to get my approval as I tutored him. When I asked him if he could collect his ideas for an essay and write an outline by the next session, he answered, "No problem."

But Lloyd was unable to do it. And for the next three weeks, he failed to complete the work that he said he could do for the next session. Each time, I started to reduce the workload, but Lloyd objected. "Really, I'm fine with this. Other things got in the way. I had less time than I thought to work."

I found out from his parents that what Lloyd had told me wasn't what was happening. He was making a strong effort, in some cases exhausting himself. His parents had pleaded with him to report how hard he'd been working. When he didn't, his parents called me. I scaled back my expectations of him and used the feedback from his parents to create a manageable workload between sessions.

Lloyd expected more from himself than he was able to deliver. The result was that his confidence in his ability to meet intellectual challenges took a hit each time he didn't meet a goal for the next tutoring session. Whether or not he knew it, his faith in tutoring was being undermined, and the pace of his improvement was being slowed. In Lloyd's case, his unrealistic expectations made tutoring less constructive for him.

Extending the Work of the Tutor Beyond the Tutoring Session

Howie, a fifteen-year-old freshman in high school, was a champion mountain biker, a boy who was never happier than when he was cruising along a trail or sailing through the air midjump. The outdoors on his bike was his home. The indoors, especially at school, was another matter.

"When his teachers look at him, they see the word 'overdue' stamped on his forehead," his father said.

In the last year, his father's sense of wonder and bemusement at his son had turned to concern. Throughout eighth grade, Howie had shown flashes of aptitude.

"Across the board, he's a pretty bright kid, or bright enough," his father said, "but there's no doubt he doesn't know how to juggle his work. What do they call that? 'Executive functioning issues'? It doesn't need a name."

Howie was chronically late with assignments in every class. Math and science had been particularly disastrous for him, because his teachers methodically subtracted points for every day overdue.

Now Howie faced ninth grade. "Yahoo!" he said bravely. His father buried his face in one hand.

Before our first meeting was over, Howie's father pulled me aside. "Look," he said, "I don't know what you have in mind, but you're not going to get anywhere with twice weekly sessions. As soon as he is out of your sight, he'll go offtrack. I think you're going to have to e-mail or phone him almost daily. Would you? We'll do our best to make sure he replies."

"Let's first see what he needs," I said.

Howie turned in his work on time for the first week and a half of the semester, but soon enough he seemed to forget the daily math assignments. I had urged him to work from a planner, writing down all of his assignments, but he kept forgetting to buy one.

As the workload ramped up, Howie struggled to keep track. I bought the planner for Howie, presenting it to him one session and watching him fill out the work he needed to do for the week. I told him to be sure that he continued to fill it in. He should keep track of what work he needed to do each day.

At our next meeting, Howie forgot to bring the planner. He brought it the following time. It was filled in, but he had still forgotten to do a math assignment and a science lab report. I asked him why.

"I entered everything in the planner earlier in the day, and then I forgot to look at it."

I decided to follow his father's suggestion. With Howie's parents pressing him to reply, the e-mails and phone calls kept him on track for nearly four weeks. He not only turned in assignments on time but he also did well in all of his classes. He'd already been above average in English and history, but now his abilities in math and chemistry began to show themselves. He was pleased.

Then came a test for him: a two-week period in which the workload was heavier. He had an exam, a quest, a science project, and a major essay in English due. Together, he and I divided up each day's work to accommodate all the work. Howie prepared reasonably well for each test and turned in his essay and his science project on time. He was late on only one daily homework assignment.

"You did well, Howie," I told him. "Now let's try to cut out the phoning or e-mailing."

"I'm not ready for that," Howie said. "Just look at me. I'm a mess." He grinned.

"I'll give you one more week," I replied. "Then I'm going to cut the phone calls and e-mails down to twice per week for two weeks. Then once per week. And then none."

"Noooo!" Howie said, clutching his chest.

Once I reduced my contact with Howie between sessions, he lapsed. In the first week, he was overdue with a math assignment and failed to turn in his history notebook for review.

Howie's father had been skeptical about his son's being prepared to take on more responsibilities. He phoned me, somewhat nervous. "He's not ready, don't you think?" he asked. "Shouldn't we go back to the old system?"

"I think we need to see how he reacts to his setbacks," I said.

At our next session, Howie took out his planner and mapped out for me all of the work of the following week without my prompting. When that week came, he had only one difficulty, an English quiz he had failed to prepare for. The week after, he turned in every assignment on time.

Over the course of another month, I ended the phone calls and e-mails.

Howie's father was partly right. Howie needed support beyond the tutoring sessions to show him how to take care of his responsibilities for every class. He needed it for a short period of time, however. Otherwise, that extra contact would teach him that I would take care of him.

The limited amount of extra contact gave Howie skills that moved him toward independence. But the expectation that it should be continued threatened to undermine his sense that he could handle his schoolwork on his own. It threatened to make him *dependent*, not *independent*.

In still other cases, it's been clear from the beginning that extra contact was the wrong thing to do. I referred earlier to a sixteen-year-old who eventually needed special remedial schooling. He not only had manipulated his past tutors into doing his work for him during sessions but also had maintained frequent contact with his tutors between sessions for any work that came up.

When he tried to do that with me, I made myself unavailable. It was clear that extra contact wouldn't have helped him. It further masked his inability to work on his own. He needed to have his teachers and parents discover just what he was unable to do so that they could determine the proper schooling for him.

Increasing the Length and Frequency of Tutoring Sessions

After six months of my working with Michael, a sophomore at a rigorous high school, he had made steady progress at writing essays. He'd learned how to collect his ideas, assess and develop them further, and organize them. He could create an outline, write a passable first draft in a reasonably quick pace, and revise his draft. Steadily, Michael's confidence in his writing had grown.

"I think I can do this now," he told me a few weeks before the end of the school year. "I don't know that I'll ever like doing this, but I can do it."

His parents had noticed the difference. "He has really come into his own," his mother said.

There was one large hurdle left: Michael's history teacher required his students to write a research paper that was due on the last day of classes of the semester. Michael had steadily read through all of his sources and assembled his ideas, but this was a larger essay than he was used to doing. It made him a little uneasy.

"You can do this. It's just a little more involved," I reassured him.

The next day, I received a phone call from Michael's mother. She reported that he was nervous about the research paper. "Would you consider staying for longer this next time? Even if it is another hour or two, we don't care. We just want Michael to be adequately supported."

I told her that I would see if that would be necessary.

During that next session, I surveyed Michael's progress. He had a relatively complete and thorough outline. I told him I thought he was in pretty good shape.

"Yeah. Maybe," he replied. "But what do I do next?"

"What do you mean?" I asked him. "You write a draft."

"Would you stay a little longer?" he asked. "Watch me write out the introduction?"

An hour later, Michael had refined the outline and completed a passable introduction. I told him he was doing fine. Then I left.

I received yet another phone call from Michael's mother the next day. She knew it was unusual, but Michael had asked her to phone me. Would I see Michael again this week? I told her that he could phone or e-mail me, but it was important for him to do the work on his own.

I never received a call. When I phoned Michael the next week to see how the paper had gone, he reported that he'd finished it without too much trouble.

If I had accommodated the request that I see Michael more often and for longer that week, it would have undermined his confidence. Michael and his mother recognized that he had progressed a great deal in the past six months. And yet the anxiety of the end of the semester—anxiety shared by both mother and son—led them to believe that he could not do this work without extra tutoring. I reassured Michael that he was capable enough by staying for extra time during our last session. He needed to see that he could write the paper by himself.

There are cases where a more frequent or longer session makes sense. Julia was a truly gifted student in some areas, but when it came to science, especially chemistry, she was a deer in the headlights, blinded and stunned at its headlong approach. Her parents were proud of her superior work in English, history, math, and Spanish.

They weren't at all fazed by her difficulties in science. Only Julia was.

"She's a little driven," Julia's mother told me, "and we want to encourage her desire to excel. We just don't want her to torture herself because she's not great in every subject."

As the end of her junior year approached, Julia was faced with a two-week period of essays, exams, and research projects that culminated with two tests in chemistry, one for the last unit and the other a final.

Julia was exhausted. "Why do I have to take chemistry at all?" she said. "I don't know how I can study for this. All this time I have to devote to doing average in it. And it makes me feel like such a cretin."

Her parents approached me. Just for these last few weeks, would I double the number of visits? I agreed. Julia wasn't going to become especially more dependent in this instance. She didn't need or want the challenges of chemistry. She just wanted to get through it. There was no expectation here that interfered with her intellectual independence.

The extra tutoring time meant only that she would concentrate well on the subject and have its key principles explained to her (once again). She would study for chemistry in ways that on her own would have taken her many more hours.

In this case, it was a good idea to extend the time together.

A Frame for Tutoring

Expectations are important and unavoidable. Some expectations undermine the process of tutoring, whereas others help it; judging which help and which hurt should occur case by case. And yet there are some kinds of commit-ments that parents, child, and tutor alike should make that are *always* necessary for the process of tutoring to succeed and that improve the odds that the right expectations will be in effect. Together, they add up to a *frame* for tutoring.

The frame is not comprehensive but rather a simple and clearly articulated set of goals and actions that stu-dent, parent, and tutor should take. The frame includes the following:

- A commitment from the parents and the student to take the long view: to measure progress not by higher grades but by the improving ability of your child to work independently and to gain a sense of competence

- A recognition that the tutor is not there to do the homework of the student but to assess and to build your child's capacities

- Clear goals for each session, such as an assignment to be done during it, and a clear sense of what the student must do between sessions

- A commitment to a regular appointment, a fee for the tutoring, terms for payment, and a policy if the student should cancel a session

The first two items in this frame dedicate tutor, stu-dent, and family to goals that go beyond a given school year or grades. They commit everyone to the habits that will make your child ultimately independent and confident.

The commitment to clear goals for each session ensures that the process of tutoring isn't divorced from the daily and weekly responsibilities of classes. It dedicates both the tutor and your child to getting the work done for school and then using that work as a means to build intellectual independence. The frame may focus on organizational issues that undermine your child's ability to work, on subject matter, or on specific habits or skills; but it does so while getting schoolwork done. In this way, the lessons of tutoring appear immediately constructive for your child's life at school.

The commitment to a regular appointment and terms of payment is equally important because it commits tutor, parent, and child to an allotted period of time at regular intervals and a fee. It establishes the time and money necessary to take the process seriously.

As simple as it may appear, this frame has the effect of creating a tutoring environment in which students can establish a relationship with the tutor and thereby develop new habits to meet old, potentially tenacious problems. It provides a context for working with your child.

Josh, a capable, shy sixteen-year-old junior at a demanding high school, was the son of an accomplished artist, an astonishingly productive and somewhat intimidating man. When it came to his schoolwork, Josh was overwhelmed by the sheer quantity of work that he was required to do and didn't see how he could focus on individual assignments, each of which seemed to be too much to do. He reacted by being tired all the time. His parents had him evaluated by a neuropsychologist. He tested well above average.

When he committed himself to a frame for organizing his efforts, a means for "parceling out" the work into manageable amounts and meeting goals for each tutoring session, he grew less tired. He began to focus on each parcel of work without the worry of the other tasks he had to perform.

He became more hopeful, too, and then more confident of his abilities. Soon enough, he was productive in the time between our sessions, so that the sessions became increasingly devoted to working intensely and well at enriching his understanding. Within three months, he cut his number of tutoring sessions in half. He ended them by the close of the school year.

When Josh committed himself to the frame for work, he found an environment in which he could remove himself from his problems with studying and set aside some of his anxieties. The frame was a practical means for producing this environment. It allowed Josh, as it allows other students, to experience his work and himself outside the dynamics with his father that had until now held him back. In the environment that tutoring created for Josh, he could more easily change habits.

Mutually agreed-upon expectations and an *appropriate frame* will help the process of making your child an independent learner. With them in place, tutoring has a substantially better chance of working on your child's difficulties profoundly. They set up the process of tutoring for success. And yet as the process of tutoring unfolds, parents are involved in an additional, vital role, reinforcing the process and providing important feedback. The nuances of that role are the subject of the next chapter.

CHAPTER THREE

Parents and Tutors

Positive Contributions and Problematic Involvement

You've decided that your child needs tutoring, selected the tutor, and established appropriate expectations for the tutoring process. Now you must find a level and type of parental involvement as your child is tutored. This chapter discusses the contributions you can make, as well as the kinds of involvement that help or hurt your child's tutoring.

Two months into our work together, Alex, a friendly, soft-spoken thirteen-year-old became unresponsive. It didn't happen overnight, but it was strange and astonishing just the same. For the first eight weeks, Alex had been attentive and hardworking as he grappled with his difficulties at reading and writing. During that time, he had made slow progress. In reading, he could now tentatively discuss themes and character development rather than simply plot in a novel. In writing, he had begun to analyze rather than simply summarize what he read.

But then came the two-month mark. Alex announced to me at our session that he was unable to complete the reading he'd been assigned for class. We had settled on this amount of work at our last meeting, so we could focus on a one-page written response that he had to do. I was puzzled. The work for the session seemed no more demanding than the work of the past few weeks.

"It was harder than I thought," Alex offered. "Sorry."

As we examined the reading he had done, I saw no sign that he had more difficulty with it than with reading he had done in the past. And yet Alex insisted it was harder when he tried to do it on his own.

"Really?" I challenged him gently. By then, I felt we were on good enough terms that I could comfortably call him out if he was being less than forthright.

"It really was," Alex said. There was something opaque about his answer. He looked down at the carpet, as if in shame. I let it go at that.

The next week, the same thing happened. Alex couldn't complete the reading before our session.

"Sorry," he said once again. "The workload in history and science has been heavy."

He explained that his teachers were all giving a lot of work right now because the quarter was almost done. They needed grades to report. In fact, he was a little behind in history, too. He had to catch up, so he had let the reading slide.

I reviewed with him how he was meeting his workload. He appeared to be making adequate time for all of his assignments. As I looked it over, the workload didn't seem any more excessive than in past weeks. I was certain that something else was going on, something he wasn't telling me.

Alex had a history research project due in two weeks. Given what had happened recently, I suggested that he start it a little earlier. I also scaled back expectations for the amount of work he should complete for each day. For our next session, I set a modest goal for research and reading.

"Does this seem doable?" I asked him.

"I can do this much," he told me.

"Sorry," he said, as we ended the session.

"You're doing what you can," I replied. "You don't have anything to apologize for."

I phoned Alex's parents to discuss his mysterious change but received only voice mail. I left a message, asking one of them to phone me back, but there was still no response.

At my next session with Alex, he told me that he had failed to turn in an English assignment—notes on a chapter of *Catcher in the Rye*—as well as complete the history work we'd discussed.

"I'm really sorry," he said yet again. "I'm trying really hard to do a good job. I'm just having a little trouble concentrating."

"Maybe you're trying too hard," I said. "Why don't you try turning in your work no matter how well you think you've done it? All you should ask of yourself is to do what you can—no more than that."

Then Alex revealed he hadn't completed the reading for either course.

"There's something wrong here," I said.

"It's just that I'm trying too hard," Alex claimed.

Again I phoned Alex's parents. Again I got their voice mail and left a message.

A week later, Alex's work ground to a halt. At that session, Alex confessed that he simply couldn't do any work.

"My parents are divorcing," he said. "There's nothing I can do about it."

Before our next session, Alex and his parents suspended tutoring.

Week after week, Alex had been a mystery, his ability to work decreasing. When he said in his last session, "There's nothing I can do about it," he showed that his schoolwork had become a casualty of his parents' divorce. He felt helpless as their marriage split apart. His upset over this event made him feel helpless to do his schoolwork as well.

Each tutoring session became a little failure for him. His regular apologies showed that he had experienced a little humiliation every session, because he could not complete assignments.

Of course, Alex's most immediate need was for counseling or the direct help of his parents, interventions that are far from what a tutor provides. Understandably, his studies suffered, and the effect of tutoring was diminished. Tutoring was of minor importance compared with what Alex was going through. (In a later chapter, I'll address tutoring students with emotional difficulties, where the parents aren't a cause, as they were for Alex.)

And yet Alex's experience speaks to an important issue for the process of tutoring any student. The end of his parents' marriage was one matter; their lack of attention to him while he was being tutored was something different.

Alex's story demonstrates how essential parental involvement can be to tutoring. Alex might have continued to improve at reading and writing during those months. In fact, developing his intellectual independence might have been truly helpful to him at a time when he was feeling pretty powerless.

For that to happen, however, Alex's parents would have to have focused more on their child's schoolwork.

Alex was unable to tell me what was making work difficult. His parents could have monitored him through these difficult times. If they had, it might have made him less distressed and more aware that his parents weren't going to abandon him because they were divorcing. It also would have contributed to a growing sense of intellectual independence. Instead, his parents' lack of involvement undercut that independence.

Positive Contributions

You don't have to be in the middle of a divorce or amid some other wrenching event for your contributions to your child's tutoring to be an important part of its success. The overwhelming majority of parents are dedicated, intelligent, and creative in their ability to help their sons or daughters, which makes them a resource well worth having for the tutor. Those contributions divide easily into two categories—*information* and *feedback*.

The Importance of Information

In tutoring as in many helping professions, the coin of the realm is *information*. A doctor may be brilliant at diagnosis, but she can be limited by the information a patient provides. A therapist's ability to succeed depends on the willingness of his patient to disclose information. Similarly, the ability of a tutor to work with your child is improved or undermined depending on the information you provide on your child's study habits and difficulties.

The reasons are simple enough. Your child may be unable to understand fully what is making matters difficult. Or your child may not want to report results that are disappointing. This is especially true as tutoring begins, when the student is just starting to feel comfortable with the tutor. So the information a student provides needs supplementing by you, the parents.

Parents should try to be comprehensive about the information they provide. In short order, followed by greater explanation, that information includes the following:

- Your child's state of mind
- Your child's study habits
- Your child's work product
- Professional advice about your child
- Observations you have from your unique perspective on your child

A Student's State of Mind. As Alex's case demonstrates, the psychological state of students makes a great difference in how they should be approached. I placed greater demands on Alex than I should have because I did not know better; I could have treated him with greater sensitivity had I known what was going on for him at home. Parents should tell tutors if they are working with a student who is experiencing emotional turbulence.

Whether it occurs for weeks or a single day, a student's state of mind can be disrupted in many ways. It doesn't take a serious trauma such as the divorce of a student's parents for this to occur. A grandparent might die or be suddenly taken away to a nursing home; a close friend might be seriously injured or in terrible trouble; a student might have lost a crucial match in field hockey or football, or failed to win a piano competition, or been denied admission to a special course for promising artists.

Anything that strongly affects the state of mind of a student is vital information for parents to tell the tutor of their child.

Study Habits. Information on study habits covers how students are completing assignments, reading, taking notes, using a planner, writing essays, and preparing for tests. It also includes how much frustration they appear to have; how focused they are as they work, especially when the work challenges them; and whether they're involved with Facebook, video games, IM'ing, or other activities far more than they let on.

The student needs to think of the tutor as different from a parent, so this information needs to be conveyed to the tutor in a manner that does not make your child feel as if she is under surveillance. If this information is delivered well, its potential effect is large.

For example, Ben was an enthusiastic kid who appeared to be baffled by his difficulties. "I go at my work every night for hours on end, but I'm still not getting this done. I have no idea why." His parents reported something entirely different. Ben would work in his room in ten-minute stretches and then come out. He had to raid the refrigerator. He just wanted to peek at the television in the living room. He needed to have a quick conversation with his younger brother about a recent upgrade in a favorite video game.

Knowing this information about Ben, I understood that he was challenged by his work or struggled with concentration far more than he confided. It made a huge difference in getting him to face his problems and get at their source, which he began to reveal once it was clear he wasn't able to study as he'd claimed.

In the Introduction, I described Peter, a student whose problems with study habits "turned out" to be related to his use of Facebook. Peter eventually admitted as much, begging me not to tell his parents, but his parents in fact made that discovery first and relayed the information to me. The information on his study habits provided by his parents accelerated Peter's progress, as it does with many students.

Work Product. Work product, too, is a critical part of what a tutor needs to examine and what a student may not always show. Parents have a role to play that strongly influences how effective the tutoring of their child will be. As much as a tutor may have a student's trust, embarrassment sometimes prevents students from reporting the results of all their work. It is essential for a parent to provide the tutor with knowledge of her child's essays, in-class writing, tests, quizzes, and any work she failed to turn in on time.

Rachel, a sixteen-year-old student I worked with, had a habit of showing me only her successful work, throwing out the disappointing results, which made it hard to review her problems. Luckily, her parents saw her doing this, fished the discarded work out of the trash, and sent it on to me. Rachel was at first angry that her parents had shown me what she'd dumped, but she slowly stopped doing it. Then she began to examine with me what had gone wrong in those cases. The information from her parents on her work allowed us to focus exactly where we needed to work.

Expert Advice. In some cases, parents have consulted experts on their child. Those experts include psychologists who have given the student a neuropsychological evaluation to test cognitive, motor, behavioral, language, and executive-functioning abilities. They also include therapists, from child or adolescent psychiatrists to social workers, who may be treating the student for behavioral issues. And they certainly include past tutors and other learning specialists who have worked with your child. (Teachers and anyone associated with the student's school are another class of experts, but that is the subject of the next chapter.)

The study habits of an eighth grader with whom I worked on organizational issues and problems in English were in utter disarray. He could not keep track of due dates, lost work repeatedly, and failed to follow his teachers' instructions with any care. I suggested that to begin with he use a planner as a kind of nerve center for keeping track of assignments and due dates.

"Makes sense," he told me in a matter-of-fact manner. Yet for two weeks, in spite of my reminders, he did not get a planner. So it went with every suggestion I made, from how to handle reading and writing to how to allot his time for preparing for a test. All of my suggestions "made sense," but he either failed to follow them or delayed acting on them for weeks if not months.

Even though his parents were up in arms, the psychologist whom the student saw was not at all surprised. "He has a great deal of trouble changing habits," she explained to me. "It's not intentional. You'll have to be patient and to keep repeating your instructions."

The advice the psychologist provided made me more understanding of the student; I adapted my style of working with him. I suggested only small changes in his study habits and then waited patiently before suggesting others. My adaptations would not have been possible without the student's parents making the psychologist available to me.

The parents may be able to pass on the expert's advice more immediately, too. Rebecca was an outgoing sixteen-year-old, articulate and seemingly filled with confidence about her abilities in virtually every subject. That, at least, is how she presented herself when I first met her. "I just need a little help in studying for tests," she told me. "They make me anxious."

Her parents cautioned me that she had many more difficulties than she was revealing. They couldn't explain them all, but they had had a neuropsychological evaluation done of her. They passed it on to me. It showed she had severe difficulties with reading, executive functioning, organization, and attention. The truth would have come out in time, but this information improved my ability to meet Rebecca's needs.

Observations. Parents also have expertise on their children that is less easily classified but often invaluable for tutors. More than anyone else, they can make observations about how their children are reacting to the tutor's instructions and recommendations. They can provide information about the ease or struggles that their children have with what the tutors urge them to do.

Students invariably have affective responses that go along with the recommendations that tutors make. Those reactions are like barometric readings: the emotional weather of the student, which can tell a tutor if he has asked too much of the student or asked too little. If a student is frustrated, confused, or overwhelmed, she might not reveal that to her tutor, especially if the tutor is new to her. The parent has the best ability to observe the student and provide the information that enables the tutor to make the proper adjustment. Think, for example, of eager-to-please Lloyd from the previous chapter. Only his parents could convey the information about him that accurately reflected how much he struggled in meeting the goals I set for him.

The Importance of Feedback

All of this information is important, but it is equally vital that parents convey to tutors how the tutor is succeeding with the student. There is no such thing as a tutor who is right for everyone. There is no such thing as a tutor whose every word or recommendation improves the rapport between him and the student. The odds that a tutor will be a good fit, however, improve substantially if the parents provide feedback on the effects the tutor is having. Tutors need to know if your child thinks the work they are doing is successful or unsuccessful.

Robert was a spirited kid with a fantastic devotion to school and to everything else in his life. Outside of school, his curiosity about geography seemed endless. Ask him about the landscape of Southeast Asia or South America, and he would take you on an adventure in books and on the Internet that could last for hours. In school, he was bright and capable in the humanities, although he struggled at remembering to complete assignments. Also, his essays showed a disorganization that suggested his forgetfulness wasn't simple absentmindedness.

When I began working with him, he was thrilled. "I really forget things," he confessed with a grin. "I could use your help." Buoyant and eager, he welcomed my suggestions for planning out his schoolwork and remembering to turn in assignments. In a short time, he improved in these areas dramatically.

We moved on to his essays. I reviewed his essays for the school year and the past year. I began to help him with a new one. In each case, I showed him ways he could harness his considerable analytical abilities in a more coherent, organized fashion. He listened intently to each suggestion and thanked me profusely for it.

Two weeks into this phase of our work, I received a phone call from his mother: Robert wasn't very happy with my suggestions. He simply disagreed with them. He didn't need help on his writing.

"He's been complaining ever since you started working on his essays with him," his mother said.

I told his mother that I thought Robert was mistaken about his essays. His teachers thought his essays needed significant improvement in the same ways I did.

But, I added, that wasn't the important matter at the moment. Robert wasn't comfortable with me. He couldn't tell me that he disagreed.

"You're right," the mother said. "He seems to have gotten it into his head that you're no longer right for him."

His mother and I discussed whether there was anything to be done. Was Robert willing to discuss this? She didn't think so. She was as puzzled as I was by his attitude. In the end, she and I agreed that I should end work with him.

I'm uncertain whether I could have helped Robert, but I'm sure that I needed to hear this feedback from his mother from the moment Robert began complaining. He was resistant to changing his habits around writing, and that led him to insist that he didn't need help. It also caused him to lose confidence that I could help him. He didn't think I was a good fit. He dug in his heels.

And yet his mother had listened to his dissatisfaction for two weeks, uncertain as to how to react and uncomfortable discussing the matter with me. During the fourteen or so days from when Robert first confided his unhappiness to his mother, his resistance to my suggestions solidified, like fast-drying concrete. If he were reachable by me, I needed to hear his complaints from the start and address them.

If your child isn't happy with his tutor, that needs to be communicated as soon as possible. Giving feedback doesn't mean parents should "rat out" their child to the tutor every time the child expresses dissatisfaction. It doesn't mean that you should effectively give your child the impression that everything she says will be communicated to the tutor. That would be counterproductive for everyone. For the tutor, it would undermine your child's sense that her relationship with her tutor is entirely distinct from her relationship with her parents, which is vital to success.

Instead, feedback means that a parent should provide the kind of insight that a student may be unable to say directly to an adult. Doing that helps the tutor remain effective. Feedback aids the developing relationship between the tutor and your child.

In the beginning weeks of my work with a somewhat nervous fourteen-year-old boy, his mother sat down with me in front of him and declared, "Samuel is worried that you're going to force yourself to be involved in everything he reads and writes. He doesn't want that to happen."

Samuel's worry was understandable even if he was far off the mark. His mother's decision to voice this in front of him and me was spot on. It showed Samuel that it was OK to voice doubts and suspicions to me. I then used that conversation to draw him out anytime he seemed to have worries about how we were working together. Slowly, he grew more comfortable and trusting of me.

Feedback also helps the tutor gauge whether the student is growing more confident of the tutor. In effect, when the tutor knows the student is happy with the tutor, he knows he's being heard well by the student. As a result, he can make bolder suggestions—calling for more sweeping changes in habits—because the student trusts the tutor's ability to lead the student in the right direction.

Problematic Involvement

Information and *feedback*—these basic elements that parents contribute to their child's tutoring—are essential in all the ways just discussed.

And yet parents are human. They don't always involve themselves well with the process of tutoring. The wrong kind of involvement inhibits the effectiveness of tutoring. It can fail to support the work of the tutor with a student. Or it can interfere with that work. There are parents who are underinvolved with their child's tutoring. There are parents who are overinvolved. And there are parents who are ambivalent about tutoring, which has its own special effect.

Underinvolved Parents

Parents who duck necessary involvement increase the chances that tutoring will fail or not succeed as well as it could. Without the proper involvement of parents, the work of tutoring will be that much more of a shot in the dark—an attempt to get at the student's problems but without critical insights.

There is no strict formula for describing underinvolvement, but consider the contrast between these two examples. The difficulties of Elizabeth, a seventeen-year-old junior in high school with severe ADHD, were utterly clear. Her abilities to explain what challenged her were excellent. She openly provided feedback. She voiced her dissatisfactions and satisfactions. She was as easy to read as the proverbial open book. It didn't matter that her parents were totally removed from the process of her tutoring. They weren't underinvolved.

But then there was Alex, the opening case of this chapter. Alex's parents were no less involved than Elizabeth's parents, but their silence made all the difference for Alex. He needed them to give voice to what he couldn't. He needed their encouragement to develop his learning abilities at a time when he was totally distracted from school.

It's easy enough to detect underinvolvement—where parents fail to supply information and feedback that they alone can provide. But in general, underinvolvement depends entirely on your child and the circumstances.

The key to figuring out whether you are involved enough is your child: Is he capable of disclosing what he needs to? Where parents do not recognize the unique needs of their child, problems occur.

That was the case with Matthew, a bright sixteen-year-old who divided his time between the homes of his parents. Matthew had slight problems that resulted from mild attention deficit order, but he was clearly a student with great ability in virtually every subject. His enthusiasm for school, however, was truly uneven. At times, he was utterly involved in his work and excited about it, bursting with intellectual interest. At other times, it seemed as if he couldn't care less.

His shifts in attitude wouldn't have mattered that much except that Matthew repeatedly failed to turn in work. There was an added complication, too: Matthew's school was astonishingly permissive. Virtually every teacher told him he could get the work in at any time. As a result, his overdue work had begun to pile up. The stage was set for matters to get quickly worse.

Matthew's mother had anticipated the problems and hired me with the consent of her ex-husband. Matthew welcomed the help, even if he didn't think there was any cause for alarm. I established a schedule for him to complete his overdue work, which he pledged to follow. Meanwhile, I kept him working on new assignments during our sessions.

For three weeks, during which he stayed mostly at his mother's home, Matthew followed the schedule. He began to catch up. As he made substantial progress, his attitude toward school began to change as well. He consistently wanted to address individual assignments. He appeared more engaged with the work and less lackadaisical.

After those three weeks, however, Matthew began to stay with his father more frequently than with his mother. His improvement seemed to continue for two weeks.

Matthew's mother was nonetheless worried. "Matthew's father doesn't think Matthew's progress in school is a big deal," she told me. "Matthew is going to have more trouble because he's staying over there." She went on to complain that she didn't have much control over her son when he was with his father.

"Would you try to be in touch with Matthew's father on a regular basis?" she asked. "Maybe then he'll monitor Matthew a little more."

Dealing with divorced parents is always tricky. Was I hearing only the mother's displeasure with her ex-husband? Was there a legitimate reason for concern? I had to be cautious not to be caught in the middle of something.

I called the father, asking if Matthew appeared to be studying most nights. "That's just my ex-wife's worry," Matthew's father said. "He's working just fine."

I thought that was the case until about three weeks later. Matthew announced that he hadn't completed overdue assignments for two weeks. He added that he'd fallen further behind in science, Spanish, and math.

I was surprised. Matthew had told me that he was continuing to make progress. "I thought you wanted to complete this work," I said. "Are you worried that you're falling further behind?"

Matthew shrugged his shoulders. "I can catch up at any time," he said.

For all the progress Matthew had made, he was now uncomfortable discussing his current circumstances with me. His occasional enthusiasm for his work was clearly gone. I plotted out with him a revised plan for making up the most recent overdue work and suggested that he make headway on some of the older overdue assignments.

"OK," he said, but he lacked conviction.

Soon enough, I received a phone call from Matthew's mother. Matthew had received academic warning notices in three subjects.

I called to discuss this development with Matthew's father. "You know," the father said, "I wasn't that good of a student. I screwed around a lot, but I did just fine with my life. Matthew doesn't have to take the same path as other kids."

It wasn't very long before Matthew's backlog of overdue assignments was overwhelming. He had to withdraw from his school. As Matthew's case demonstrates, underinvolved parents can be poisonous. They can seriously hinder if not destroy an effort to make a student intellectually independent.

Overinvolved Parents

As sobering as Alex's and Matthew's cases are, the more common problem parents present for tutoring is overinvolvement. That's because parents tend more often to care a lot rather than too little about their child's education.

They want to do all they can to help tutoring work. They recognize that their child needs to develop the capacities to learn independently. They typically contribute well to the process of tutoring. And yet some parents make tutoring a lot more confusing and less effective.

Typically, overinvolvement comes in one of two forms:

1. The parent participates too much in the student's tutoring.

2. The parent judges the student's progress excessively.

Overparticipation. Lucinda was a nervous and shy thirteen-year-old who devoted herself to being as good a student as she could. Her school referred Lucinda and her mother to me for extra help with writing, which her mother eagerly agreed to.

"Lucinda is a bright kid," her mother told me, "a very bright kid. But she's not living up to her abilities. I'm concerned. She works hard, but she needs a lot of help from me when she writes."

Lucinda's mother handed me writing that Lucinda had submitted to her English and history classes. Lucinda's essays were extremely disorganized. Her paragraphs were factual observations in random order. Topic sentences rarely existed or were clustered into a single paragraph rather than located with their respective subtopics.

In spite of these fundamental problems, the grammar and punctuation of her essays were nearly perfect. Here and there, Lucinda's writing contained sentences that were simply elegant.

"Lucinda is a pretty intelligent reader," the coordinator of learning specialists at her school explained. "Her mother thinks she is brilliant. We haven't seen that, at least not yet. But for some reason she struggles with writing. Her English teacher has spent a lot of extra time with her."

I began my work with Lucinda by emphasizing the difference between ideas and facts. She was capable of distinguishing them. I carefully explained how to write a paragraph by marshaling facts in support of an idea. I suggested that for now, she should begin a paragraph with the idea and then use the supporting facts to explain it.

"Do you understand this?" I asked her.

Lucinda said she did. We practiced creating a paragraph in this way. She got it, it seemed, although her confidence was shaky.

"Is this right?" she asked repeatedly.

Given her uneasiness, I decided that we should create an elaborate outline for an essay draft she had due in a few weeks. It should spell out a thesis. It should identify ideas for the topic sentences of each paragraph. Below those ideas, there should be supporting ideas and evidence after it. In effect, the outline would provide an extremely clear picture of how to structure each paragraph. We worked on preparing this outline for two sessions.

At the end of those sessions, I told her to use this outline as a road map for creating a draft of her essay. It would keep her focused as she wrote.

"Wait," Lucinda said, suddenly anxious. "I don't get it. How am I going to write good sentences from this?"

"First, write a draft by following the outline," I told her. "Try to connect your ideas and facts. Then we'll address your sentences."

A few days later, Lucinda e-mailed me a draft from the outline we'd worked on together. The draft bore almost no resemblance to the outline. It was as if she had abandoned the outline altogether and reverted to the same rat's nest of prose that characterized the samples of her writing that her mother had given me.

And yet every sentence was grammatical and well punctuated. The draft was also studded with sentences that were truly well crafted for a thirteen-year-old. In fact, they struck me as far too advanced for Lucinda.

"Did you follow the outline, Lucinda?" I asked her when we met.

"My mom did it with me," she answered.

The next day, I received a phone call from her mother. "Lucinda had a lot of trouble following this outline," she told me, "so I helped her with the draft. I hope you don't mind."

It isn't unusual for a parent to help a child prepare an essay, but in this case I had my suspicions that the mother's help had taken on an added dimension. I asked her mother if she would let Lucinda write a new draft of the essay all by herself, following the outline. I needed to see exactly what Lucinda could do.

"I'll try," Lucinda's mother said. "It's hard. She really has a difficult time."

I wondered exactly whose difficulty the mother was referring to.

This time, Lucinda's essay draft came back with an argument that followed the outline nearly to the letter. It was a vast improvement. The sentences within the essay were another matter. Many were ungrammatical. She misused commas constantly. There was no evidence of the occasional, elegant sentences from the past.

That same day, Lucinda's mother phoned again. "See what I mean?" she told me. "She's got real writing problems. It was hard not to jump in and fix things."

It took a little time, but I eventually persuaded Lucinda's mother that this draft was progress. Fixing the individual sentences could wait. In fact, teaching Lucinda to write better sentences would be easier once the larger issues of creating a well-organized argument were solved. Eventually, her mother stopped editing Lucinda's work.

Lucinda's writing problems belonged not simply to her but also to her overinvolved mother. Her mother's fixation on writing good sentences had diverted Lucinda from learning the fundamentals of a good essay. Lucinda had tried to practice what I'd shown her. Her mother had taken over.

Lucinda was able to improve once her mother's involvement changed. Her mother's intentions were honorable. She was anxious for her daughter's success, so she had adopted what some people call the "helicopter mode." She hovered over Lucinda as her daughter studied, intervening at the first sign her daughter had difficulty. She was a friendly, well-meaning helicopter. But for Lucinda, whose confusions were real, the mother's efforts were a problem. Another child might have overcome her mother's misguided directions. Here, the parent's involvement sabotaged the efforts of tutor and teacher.

All of this resulted from good intentions: good intentions are not enough to justify every kind of involvement that a parent has with her child's tutoring.

Excessive Judgments. The beginning of my sessions with Alan resembled criminal court. There was Alan, an amiable, mischievous fifteen-year-old, his head slightly bowed. Before him was his father, the prosecutor. I was the reluctant jury.

"So this week," Alan's father would begin, "Alan not only failed to turn in his work in history, but we got a note from his science teacher. He hasn't turned in a lab report that was due more than a week and a half ago."

Alan was an average to above-average student who had genuine problems with executive functioning. He'd made steady, slow improvements over the past semester. I'd gotten him to use a planner consistently. He'd cut down the number of assignments he'd missed to only a few. Apparently, however, during a crunch time earlier in the month, he'd forgotten some work.

This was unforgivable so far as Alan's father was concerned.

"It's not the grades," he said. "I've said that before. It's just he's got to make an honest effort and own up to what he's doing."

"I'm not being dishonest," Alan muttered.

Alan's father glared at him. "You're in the doghouse." He left Alan and me to work.

"Woof," Alan said when his father was gone.

Slowly, over the course of that session, Alan talked about what had happened about five weeks earlier. It had been a tough week: two tests and an essay due. He'd realized he'd forgotten to hand in the lab report about three days later.

"Why didn't you say anything to me?" I asked.

"I didn't want to get in trouble. And then I forgot about it. There was all this other work I had to do."

I knew what trouble Alan meant: his father's displeasure at the news. But then I'd never caused Alan this kind of trouble. In fact, I'd strictly avoided giving such reports to Alan's father because he was so volatile. What's more, I'd asked him not to discipline his son in front of me.

Alan knew as much, but it didn't matter. I'd become associated with his father. His father's involvement in Alan's tutoring had compromised Alan's ability to disclose to me what was happening with his schoolwork.

Eventually, I managed to persuade Alan's father to leave me out of his tirades. Alan began to come around. He began to reveal more of how he tripped himself up while trying to manage his assignments. I was able to create solutions. It took months longer than it might have.

Looking back at this story, one can see a clear case of an overinvolved parent. Alan's father was deeply interested in helping his son, but he believed that the solution was to intervene in his son's studies in a forceful and sometimes punitive way. He included me in his attempt. Never mind that he probably had been acting this way toward Alan long before they hired me. Never mind that this style of approaching Alan hadn't worked.

The net effect was to cause Alan to hide more of his problems and to damage my ability to establish rapport with him—a relationship that was distinct from that of Alan's father. Alan needed to believe he was in a neutral space when he worked with me. He needed that neutral space to investigate his current habits and establish new ones. The constant judgment of his father interfered with the process of tutoring developing such a space.

This kind of excessive judgment of a student sometimes occurs sight unseen to a tutor, but it has a similar effect. George was a seventeen-year-old at a well-regarded high school in New York. His work was average at best, in spite of the extraordinary potential he showed through testing and through flashes of ability that virtually every one of his teachers had noticed.

George's parents, an advertising copywriter and a graphic designer, appeared friendly in front of George. They were affectionate with him, yet they lightly ribbed him about his difficulties. At times, they appeared more comfortable in the role of George's buddies than in the role of mother and father.

Alone with George, I found that he expressed genuine interest for what he learned at school, but in small doses only. As soon as he expressed enthusiasm, he'd follow it with some glib statement dismissing his enthusiasm. He was deeply interested in Nietzsche's ideas of the Apollonian and the Dionysian. Then he remarked about his interest, "Well, look at that. There's some deep thinking there."

George was consistently friendly, the proverbial hail-fellow. It felt like a mask. A few months into my work with him, the mask came off. During that session, he told me that he was sick of studying even though he hadn't been working all that hard. He also confided that he had been fighting a lot with his parents about his efforts at studying.

"Don't believe their jokester style," he said. "Fighting is our routine. I fight with them, go to sleep, wake up, and fight again. It gives a whole new meaning to marathon sports."

I asked him if he liked to learn. He said that of course he did. It was a kind of refuge for him from his parents. I asked him why he was sick of studying, then.

He had a simple answer: "Because they're always after me to do it. I'm tired of doing what they want me to do."

It took a long time before George could think of tutoring as a place where he could build intellectual abilities for himself, but eventually he did and our tutoring sessions proved valuable to him.

Ambivalent Parents

There is one more problematic involvement worth addressing: the ambivalent parent. Matthew's father, in the section on underinvolved parents, was ambivalent about school. The ambivalence described in this section is about tutoring itself. It appears in both the actions and the words of the parents who don't really believe tutoring is worth much or at least as much as they're paying for it. Their child then picks up on this attitude and learns not to value what happens in tutoring.

Cressida was a lively senior in high school who had struggled through history classes. As hard as she'd prepare, every history test seemed to go badly for her. On the phone, her parents declared to me that "nothing is more important than our daughter"—as if I were being warned. I scheduled an initial assessment of Cressida, asking her to collect her notes, her tests, and all of the materials she had prepared to study for them.

Our first meeting included Cressida and her mother. Cressida was a serious, intent seventeen-year-old who had carefully assembled all that I'd asked of her. Her mother was easygoing and friendly but seemingly scattered. During our meeting, she repeatedly answered her cell phone, only to tell whoever was on the phone, "I'm in a meeting. I'll call you back."

My assessment did not take long. Cressida was extraordinarily well organized and dedicated to her studies; and yet she was being defeated by her poor study habits. For each test, she prepared a study guide that copied every fact, concept, and term her class had studied for the unit. She wrote down nearly all of the information in the assigned chapters of her history book and primary documents. But she had no means of condensing what she learned.

"I think you study very hard," I told her, "but you lack a way of filtering the information and concepts the course requires. Not everything is as important as everything else. I think I can help you make choices that will make this easier and less frustrating."

"That makes a lot of sense," she replied. She looked relieved.

I told her that although I didn't know for sure, I thought that a short amount of tutoring would help her.

As we parted, Cressida's mother said to me (before her daughter could say anything), "She seems genuinely pleased. I guess she thinks this will help."

We agreed to begin work the following week.

A day later, I received a phone call from Cressida's mother. "This is awkward," she said. "I don't like bringing this up, but I have to, I think."

I encouraged her to speak her mind.

"Well, I couldn't help noticing that you seemed to smirk as you spoke to my daughter. As if you found what she had done to study kind of funny."

"Smirk?" I said.

"Yes, I'm sure you didn't mean it. But it was upsetting."

I answered that I didn't think I'd been smirking, that it would have been inappropriate to do that.

"I'm sure you didn't mean it," Cressida's mother repeated. "I don't think Cressida saw it, but I did. That's why I brought it up with her."

"If she thinks I did that, she must be upset," I said.

"She was briefly, but she's OK now."

I asked if I should speak with Cressida, but her mother said everything was OK now. I hung up the phone wondering what had just happened.

A week later, I began work with Cressida. She was considerably more reserved than when I had first seen her. I tried to draw her out by focusing on the work. I showed her how to identify only the most important concepts and historical developments for her next test and to limit her study of facts and dates to those she associated with them.

At the end of the session, I asked her if this way of going about studying seemed simpler.

"I'm not dumb," she said. "I get it."

I looked at her. "No one thinks you're dumb, Cressida," I said.

"OK," she said. "I have to go now."

Two days later, Cressida's mother phoned to say that Cressida believed she could handle preparing for tests just fine now without me.

This strange little story is both typical and atypical. It's typical in that it shows how a parent's mixed feelings about tutoring can undermine it entirely. That ambivalence quickly translates into doubt or reluctance in the student.

The story is atypical for how this ambivalence appeared and how swiftly it destroyed an opportunity for tutoring to help Cressida. Her mother saw a smirk in me because she needed to see a smirk. She needed to torpedo tutoring because she was uncomfortable with it for some reason that was not clear to me. Her effort worked. It would have been better for her daughter, who was a little wounded in the process, if she hadn't sought tutoring at all.

I've encountered parents who are ambivalent about the commitment to tutoring, so they phone to cancel sessions a few weeks at a time or ask for impossible, last-minute changes in the dates and times. I've tried to accommodate their changes, but eventually I refused to hold a specific appointment open for the student when the cancellations became regular. In a related, less-classifiable case, a parent insisted that she wanted me to help her eighteen-year-old high school senior, but she wanted my work with her son to be hidden from her disapproving husband, who was equally involved in his child's life. Eventually, I convinced her to give up on tutoring rather than pursue it in secret. Still other parents have complained about the expense and have attempted to pay a discounted fee even though the money I charged was clearly not a burden for them.

The contributions and involvement of parents are vital elements in the success of tutoring. The content and style of parental involvement should be geared to the unique needs of their child. You have the ability to make the tutoring of your child powerful by providing the right information and feedback in a timely manner and style. You also have the ability to make it underwhelming and even damaging in its effect. The Introduction and the last three chapters have focused on how to make the right choices. Next, we turn to the relationship tutors have with your children's school—especially their teachers.

CHAPTER FOUR

Teachers and Tutors

You're doing all that you can to ensure that tutoring is successful. Your child and tutor are working well together. But there is another very important relationship the tutor must negotiate, and this is with your child's teachers. This chapter outlines the kind of relationships parents should expect tutors to cultivate with teachers. It also suggests ways that tutors can help students resolve their own problems with teachers.

The past few chapters have focused on the relationships between tutor, student, and parents. Now we need to turn to the relationship between tutors and teachers. Should tutors have a relationship with your child's teachers? If so, what kind? There are no simple answers to these questions. Once again, parents should evaluate what is best case by case. And yet there are several common issues you should be aware of as you decide whether a tutor should be in or out of touch with your child's teachers.

How Tutors Can Reach Out to Teachers

Fourteen-year-old Winthrop didn't want to admit he needed help of any kind, even if he'd flunked French and nearly flunked English the past school year. "I can take care of this myself," he told me when I first met him.

"You don't want to be tutored?" I asked him.

"Maybe not," he said. "I haven't made up my mind."

I asked Win what had caused his problems the previous year.

"Aren't you supposed to help me figure that out?" Win replied. "Not that I've decided to do this."

After a push from his parents, Win reluctantly agreed to let me help.

An ambivalent student is rarely easy. Win was true to form. As the school year began, he occasionally withheld information about what assignments he had due, "forgot" his schoolbooks or assignments when we met, and otherwise obstructed my ability to help him.

He was equally adept at keeping his parents in the dark. And still they continued to insist he be tutored even if I openly questioned whether he was ready for it.

"He'll come around," they advised, "Please don't give up. Please stay with it."

Slowly, Win shared more of his assignments with me. His overall workload continued to seem light, and at times, I stumbled on completed work for assignments he'd failed to mention. So I knew he wasn't showing me everything his teachers had assigned to be done. With all this secrecy, his first-quarter progress report was naturally a surprise: solid work in math and science but an incomplete in English because he failed to turn in several assignments; a warning in history for unspecified reasons; and a cryptic note from his French teacher: "There is some cause for concern, but I need to think about this."

I asked Win why he hadn't told me of his difficulties in three courses.

"Because it's kind of fun," Win said. He grinned.

Until this point in the school year, Win's parents did not want me to have contact with the school, even though I'd suggested a few times that it might help.

"We'd just prefer that you not get involved with them," Win's mother had said. But when Win's progress report for the quarter appeared, they changed their minds.

Making First Contact

Via e-mail and phone, I reached out to Win's English, history, and French teachers. His English teacher, Ms. Kessler, responded first. She explained that she typically challenged the students from the very start of the semester. This semester was no different. She had assigned a fair amount of reading for each class, asked students to answer questions daily on each reading assignment, quizzed them weekly to assess comprehension, and required them to keep journals for reactions to readings. She also gave the students an in-class essay assignment and one longer essay to prepare. I was aware of about half of these assignments.

Ms. Kessler also provided key insights into Win: he was cooperative and making a truly energetic attempt, but he was clearly struggling. I was struck by the difference between Win the perpetual resistor in tutoring and Win the student at school. It couldn't have been more stark a contrast.

"He can get better at it. I think he's lost when he reads literature," she explained. "It's mostly a swarm of words for him, with a discernible plot. He's intelligent, but he needs some basic help to catch up with the rest of the class. Are you open to suggestions?" she asked me.

I told her of course I was.

She asked if we could use my tutoring to leverage any instruction she provided, and when I agreed, she said, "Please try to work with him on reading comprehension first. Leave the writing assignments alone. Let's get him equipped to read first. Then we can address his writing."

Meanwhile, Win's history teacher responded to me in a distinctly different way. He reported that Win was abrasive, defiant, and minimal in his efforts. The teacher was more than exasperated with Win.

"He knows what he has to do. He can do it. You should tell the parents that I'm not above flunking him, and they should contact me."

I asked him what if anything he'd like me to focus on with Win.

"Anything else I'll explain directly to his parents," the teacher replied curtly. "On general principle, I don't care much for tutoring."

Win's French teacher never replied to any of my e-mails or phone calls.

Positive Results

My contact with Win's English teacher helped Win. His reading comprehension began to improve. As it did, Win began to be more engaged in class and dutiful about completing the assignments. Slowly, he stopped denying that he had work due and readily volunteered where he needed help.

Ms. Kessler's insights and information helped Win's work not only in English but also in history. Although some antagonism between the history teacher and Win certainly was a factor, I suspected that his reading difficulty had led to Win's misbehavior in class and inadequate work on some assignments. As I focused Win on reading comprehension in history, his attitude toward class changed just enough that the warnings from his history teacher ended. His problems in French class disappeared as well. Win reported that his French teacher was a little bizarre, but he had been paying "better attention." To this day, it is unclear why things improved in French, but I suspect there was some kind of associative effect as his confidence grew in his other problem courses.

How Tutors Should Relate to Teachers

My contact with Win's teachers identifies a range of important, general factors and goals affecting the relationship between teachers and tutors. They include the following:

- The exchange of valuable information
- The importance of the tutor following the teacher's instructions
- The attempt to overcome communication problems between tutors and teachers

The Exchange of Valuable Information

Win's English teacher made comments and requests that show how the exchange between teacher and tutor can positively affect the learning of a student in both the classroom and tutoring—"both" because the teacher and tutor may not be pursuing the exact same goals. The tutor may be working on only a piece of what the teacher covers, such as writing. Or the tutor's duties may extend beyond the individual course, as mine did in this case.

The English teacher and I built a loose alliance directed at meeting the first of several goals for Win, in this case, reading comprehension. This exchange led to a more coherent, simple plan for helping Win in spite of his maddening resistance to tutoring and self-destructive response to his difficulties in Ms. Kessler's class.

Win needed remedial work in reading. Although he had native intelligence, he lagged behind his classmates at this fundamental skill. That alone was a large reason for his feeling lost in the classroom, as well as his failure to complete assignments.

Ms. Kessler's comments led me to redirect my attention appropriately and made my work as a tutor quickly more constructive. They also changed Win's openness to tutoring—so far as English was concerned. As a result, Win progressed.

Teacher's insights are invaluable for what they reveal about a student's learning difficulties. They lead the tutor to focus more quickly on how to help the student. Ms. Kessler recognized as much when she offered comments. She also recognized my benefit for her efforts with Win. Unlike the teacher, the tutor has far more individual time for instructing the student. The tutor can do things to develop the student's abilities in the classroom that the teacher most often hasn't the time to do.

In some cases, the teacher's insights are more like clues than usable conclusions about what is going on with the student. I had another sixteen-year-old student I tutored for work in sociology and writing. He was pleasant and attentive in our sessions, but the teacher reported that he was consistently disruptive in class. Time and again, as the teacher instructed the class, this student would hold a conversation with his neighboring student, no matter whom he was sitting near.

I explored this disruptive behavior with him. It turned out to be a sign of problems that he had in processing information that was not written out or represented graphically. Whenever the teacher addressed the class without the benefit of the blackboard or any other visual aid, the student quickly grew confused and acted out.

The teacher's observations provided the grounds for my figuring this out. In turn, it led to changes in the student's behavior in his sociology class and beyond, once we'd created habits for the student to take in lessons that were exclusively in spoken form.

The tutor not only receives but also gives valuable information or observations to teachers. I had a thirteen-year-old student who appeared disengaged and disrespectful to her science teacher. I knew from tutoring that she was embarrassed by her inability to understand and was reluctant to approach the teacher. In fact, she didn't want to reveal to anyone, even her parents, that she was having difficulty with science assignments that involved inductive reasoning. But the real reason for her behavior became clear in tutoring. From our one-on-one work, I knew that she was intense and demanding of herself. She would cringe when she made mistakes and sometimes fret that she should be able to do this. It wasn't hard to understand that her behavior in class was related to her tendency to be critical of her abilities and impatient with her development.

I passed on to the teacher a report of the student's reactions in tutoring and her despair over her science difficulties. The teacher then changed her approach to the student. The net result was astonishing: the student transformed herself into one of the better students in the class.

Tutors can provide more than interpretation of behavior to teachers. I have had teachers who had never been informed that a student had organizational difficulties and other problems that greatly affected how the student should be taught. Once the teacher had that information, the student quickly became better adjusted to the class and developed more easily.

In another case, I had a student with complicated writing difficulties, for whom I provided a precise and methodical approach to writing. The teacher learned of this approach from me and coordinated her instruction to this student with my own. Once our approaches to the student were comparable, the student began to show improvement.

My interaction with Win's English teacher was also an exchange. Shortly after I began to focus on reading comprehension, Win showed that he accelerated past any parts of a text that presented him with difficulty. I slowed him down as he read and alerted her to this strategy. As a result, when she called on him in class, she too slowed him down, and with our joint effort his reading greatly improved.

Following the Teacher's Instructions

The exchange of valuable information is one part of what occurs between teacher and student. Yet another element to consider is whether a tutor takes cues and follows instructions from the teacher as he tutors. In Win's case, I did what his English teacher asked of me. It helped that I agreed with her sense that the first priority for Win was reading comprehension, but my agreement wasn't what was most important. Reinforcing the tactics of the teacher was. Following the teacher's lead accelerated Win's understanding and faith in the teacher, and it reduced his opposition to me.

If the work of the tutor involves the classroom directly, the tutor should in most cases go along with what the teacher wants. Doing so furthers the student's intellectual independence. A student needs to adjust to the learning style of the school as quickly and fully as possible. The teacher's classroom couldn't be more central to that adjustment. Following the teacher's instructions will help the tutor focus on interpreting the classroom style of a course for the student, hastening the student's ability to understand and to flourish in that class.

In some cases, the tutor translates the teacher's instructions into a language for learning that the student more readily understands—until the student gains fluency in the teacher's language. For example, one student I was tutoring needed help interpreting her history teacher's essay assignments and examinations. She persistently failed to address all that was being asked of her until I gave her a method for analyzing the teacher's instructions and encouraged her to be more proactive about asking the teacher what was being demanded.

There are of course exceptions. I've had students who struggled to understand a teacher's style of instruction in spite of consistent effort. A fifteen-year-old student of mine was particularly methodical in his learning style. He needed step-by-step instructions to approach a topic. He had a teacher of English and American poetry who wanted students to react impulsively. His teacher wanted him to free-associate spontaneously to the poems they were reading. She provided excellent suggestions for interpreting poetry, but they weren't in any apparent order. The student had persistent difficulties. The teacher went out of her way to spend extra time with the student, but he simply couldn't get poetry as she taught it.

In his case, I provided an alternative approach that involved building an interpretation of a poem through a combination of line-by-line paraphrasing and a thorough examination of diction, imagery, tone, and figures of speech. It was as far from an impulsive reaction as one could get, but the step-by-step quality of this approach fit his learning style. Meanwhile, I kept his teacher informed of how I'd helped him. She was gracious but a little annoyed; concerned that he wouldn't have any visceral reaction to the poems. In time, however, she reported that he was doing fine. The comfort of a more methodical approach to the poems allowed the student to connect with what he read.

There are still other examples where the tutor should not follow the lead of the teacher. In cases where the student and teacher consistently clash with each other, following the teacher's lead in some obvious way could make the student less willing to be helped. It could also make the student associate the tutor with the teacher too much.

The matter should be decided case by case. Parents should expect the tutor to establish clear, productive communication with teachers when it benefits their children. Those potential benefits include supporting the learning style of their student's classroom, thereby accelerating their children's abilities to adjust to school.

Overcoming Communication Problems Between Tutors and Teachers

Tutors will sometimes find communicating with teachers to be difficult. Consider the range of responses to me from Win's teachers: Ms. Kessler was certain that I could help and primed to use me. His history teacher greeted me as if I were a Cold War enemy. As for the French teacher, who knows? She may have shared the history teacher's attitude, perceived no use for a tutor, or felt no obligation to respond.

At the very least, these responses identify mixed reactions to the presence of a tutor. It is important for parents to be aware of why this may be the case. For one thing, there is a real fear that the tutor may be acting inappropriately. In a culture where grade competition is emphasized, teachers sometimes suspect that tutors are doing the work for the students. They have concerns that your child's advancement is not so much his or her own but that of the tutor.

It may not be explicit, but teachers sometimes note that the student's in-class work is nowhere near the quality of the work done out of school. So they think the student is getting unfair help, which undermines the teacher's ability to evaluate the student's abilities and needs.

For example, I had an energetic, dutiful student whom I tutored in writing. Lamarcus, a fifteen-year-old, was intelligent but utterly at sea about how to get his thoughts onto paper. I had him work quite hard to correct his difficulties. For an essay on Henrik Ibsen's *Doll's House*, I had Lamarcus prepare extensive notes, three versions of an outline that grew increasingly detailed, and three drafts of an essay.

When his teacher read the essay, she called him in for a brief conference. She asked him flatly whether this was his work. He was baffled by his teacher's response and said, "Yes, of course it is."

Eventually I spoke with the teacher. By the end of the conversation, she was somewhat convinced that the student had written the essay. Only somewhat. She asked that I no longer work with the student on any pending assignments—only on work that had already been completed.

The effect of his teacher's response on Lamarcus was subtle but clear. His feeling of achievement, his growing sense that he could with effort and with a clear sense of a writing process become a competent writer, was shaken. Ultimately, Lamarcus overcame the experience. He realized that whatever suspicion his teacher may have had, he had in fact done the work. That had everything to do with his feeling better about his abilities to learn independently. For other students, overcoming such an experience is more difficult.

So teachers sometimes suspect that tutors are doing the work for students. They also have mixed reactions to tutors out of a sense of fairness. Teachers worry that the students who have tutors are only the wealthier ones (yet another way in America that money gives a leg up to those students who have it). They worry that tutoring gives the students with every advantage still more advantages.

These two concerns go to the heart of what should be the mutual goals of teacher and tutor, goals that education in the United States is trying to meet: first, that education develops the capacity of students to think and express themselves on their own; and second, that education provides equal opportunity.

So understandably, the teacher may resent the tutor. Win's mother was initially reluctant that I be in contact with the school, because she worried that I would not be well received and that her son would come under suspicion for using a tutor.

It doesn't have to be this way, but parents should be aware of these nuances. Tutors should be utterly committed to enabling students to do the work. And as the final chapter will address, quality tutoring should be made available to everyone—a responsibility that falls on many shoulders, including tutors'.

Meanwhile, where appropriate, tutors should cultivate relationships with teachers. They should reinforce the lessons of the classroom, gain information on the habits of the student that prove useful to tutoring, and provide teachers with information on the student to facilitate the teacher's ability to work with the student.

The Importance of Selective Contact

So far, this chapter has addressed circumstances where tutors cultivate contact with schools. And yet there are circumstances where contact with teachers and the school should be minimal, where the tutor should be "out of touch" or maintain a discreet distance.

By out of touch, I don't mean that tutors should be secretive about what they are doing. Instead, the contact may be modest or nonexistent, because in a specific situation, such contact might be intrusive or decrease the ability of tutoring to build intellectual independence.

The Importance of a Discreet Distance

Here, for example, is the story of William, a fifteen-year-old freshman at an above-average public high school in Manhattan. William was the son of a sound technician and a community activist. His parents had created a happy if slightly chaotic home for him and his younger sister.

William was animated and charming, with many friends and admirers. He was also a truly intelligent kid but with an erratic track record as a student. Each year, as if on cue, he seemed to have difficulty with at least one teacher. In seventh grade, he nearly flunked history because he took a dislike to the teacher. In eighth grade, he barely passed science class. There was plenty of evidence that William was a good student in math and science and almost as capable in humanities.

Then came his first semester in ninth grade. The stakes were higher because he wanted to build a record for college. And still William couldn't resist his tendencies when he discovered the injustices (in his view) of his French teacher, Madame Boese.

William had been diagnosed with pronounced ADHD, so he was supposed to be given extra time on tests. He told Madame Boese that he was to receive extra time, and yet Madame believed that William didn't need it. She told him that he should complete the exam in the specified amount of time and stop pretending to be, in her words, "disabled."

Madame's response infuriated William. So the son of a community activist mounted his own, dysfunctional form of protest—a private strike, which he began with that test. He manned the ramparts. He raised his banner. He stormed the barricades. Or, as he proudly related to me, "I got to a certain point in the exam and then just stood up and walked out of the classroom."

Madame Boese reported him for cutting class that day and gave him an F on the exam. William responded in kind: he stopped turning in assignments.

"If she wasn't going to respect me," William said, "I wasn't going to respect her class."

Next, Madame Boese began serving William up with a flurry of academic warnings, one after another within the course of five weeks. After those warnings, with his parents leaning on him, William turned in the remaining assignments for the semester.

He also went back and completed the overdue work for those five weeks. On each one of the overdue assignments, his teacher wrote out a grade designating what William would have received if the work had been turned in on time. (Typically, they were B's or C's.) Then Madame crossed out the B or the C and marked down the assignment to a D- because it was *"trop en retard"* (too late). William barely passed that semester. His grade was a D.

With William's agreement, I was hired to help.

"It's only going to get worse," he warned. "Rumors are that Madame Boese isn't coming back next year. She's been fired."

Then he made a very different kind of comment: "I'd really like to learn French. I really have trouble with all the memorizing and things. But this teacher . . . "

This story had a happier ending than William had anticipated. He managed to improve substantially in this class, but it didn't result from my extensive contact with the teacher. In fact, it was important that I kept my distance.

William liked to get into it with teachers. By his own account, that was his track record. Mixing it up with teachers was nearly a point of honor for him. The further I stayed away, the more likely it was that I wouldn't be caught up in the antagonistic relationship he'd created with Madame Boese.

If I had been in contact with Ms. Boese, William would have constantly asked me whether Ms. Boese was awful and whether he was being mistreated. I would have been asked to be judge or jury, which wouldn't have helped William to adapt to his circumstances. He had parents and administrators to act as jurors and judges.

Instead, my focus was on William's work in French and his ability to learn from this teacher. Virtually the only source of information I had about this class and this teacher was William himself. It was William's reactions to the teacher, William's tendencies each school year to dislike one teacher, and William's interesting comment about his difficulty in French that were my concern.

The teacher may or may not have mistreated William, but more important, William revealed that he had some struggles with memorization in French. His attraction to fighting with teachers was a handy distraction from getting at those problems. And hidden within William's stormy relationship with Madame Boese was the genuine possibility that she could teach him some French and even address his problems.

In fact, on closer inspection, I discovered that William's problems weren't simply in memorizing all the vocabulary but rather in sorting out differences in verb tense and understanding the subjunctive. Keeping away from William's teacher enabled me to stay focused on helping him to learn French. It had allowed me to model for William a way of paying attention to learning in spite of his likes or dislikes of the teacher.

Perhaps it needs to be said: there are bad teachers. There are lazy teachers. There are inconsistently good teachers. There are burnt-out teachers. But the overwhelming majority of teachers are neither bad nor lazy. They work hard for relatively little money, because they want students to learn; and they go out of their way to devote extra time to making that happen.

In the case of William's French teacher, it doesn't matter whether his accusations had merit or whether he deserved to be treated severely. For the tutor, the important matter here was not to take sides in such apparent disputes but to help the student learn because of or in spite of the teaching style of the teacher. This wouldn't be the last time that William would have a conflict with a teacher or professor. My role was to teach the student to learn in spite of his attitude toward the teacher.

There's an additional reason for keeping distance between tutor and teacher. The student may change his or her mind and recognize opportunities that the teacher provides. Also students don't always mean exactly what they say when expressing their dislike of a teacher. It could be a lack of interest in a subject. It could be a particular difficulty with that subject. It could be a difficulty with the intellectual demands the teacher is placing on the student.

Whatever the case, the student is capable of changing attitudes, so it's best for the tutor to remain neutral and to make the tutoring environment neutral in judgment. In this way, the student is freer to change his mind. He also learns more about the variety of reactions he has to teachers, including why he reacts as he does and how his attitude is capable of changing.

As examples of what I mean, consider two different kinds of teachers that a student reported to me. I'll refer to them as the *disorganized teacher* and the *underutilized teacher*. I have no reason to believe or disbelieve the student's account of these teachers. That is entirely beside the matter. The point is to address how a student learns to learn in the differing environments that teachers establish in their classrooms and by their style of instruction.

This does not mean that a student must be compliant in every circumstance within school. It means only that parents should expect the tutor to enable the student to learn from any teacher—without expectation of intervention or need to change the teacher or school.

The (So-Called) Disorganized Teacher

Mr. Higginbotham was a wonderful art history teacher as far as Robbie, a seventeen-year-old junior, was concerned. Robbie explained that Mr. H. was enthusiastic and passionate about the subject, and he was also *so* cool. A gifted student of art and film, Robbie was excited about an academic subject for the first time in my experience with him. He credited Mr. Higginbotham for it. Robbie was undoubtedly talented in art history, but he also had severe problems with executive functioning, which meant that he had a great deal of difficulty keeping on top of all of his tasks.

That turned out to be true in art history as well. As the year went on, Mr. H. continued to be a great guy and a great teacher so far as Robbie was concerned; but he became more "annoying," too. He did not seem to care if Robbie turned in work late, Robbie reported. He made it hard for Robbie to know exactly what was due and when it needed to be handed in. When the first semester ended, Mr. Higginbotham gave Robbie an incomplete. Robbie was incensed.

From my perspective, it didn't matter if Mr. Higginbotham was indeed disorganized and more inflexible about deadlines than he appeared. What mattered was that Robbie needed to adapt to the circumstances. Whatever the experience of the class was, I needed to help him come to terms with it. I did so by holding him as best as possible to a rigorous system of recording tasks and completing them on a daily basis, as well as contacting Mr. Higginbotham via e-mail to clarify what was due when.

I repeatedly placed the responsibility on Robbie. He did his best to write down the assignment as soon as it was given out. At the end of each class, he tried to check on whether he had the assignment correctly. When he was uncertain of what the assignment was, he reached out to other students if not to Mr. H. That led to a more involved, interesting communication with Mr. H., who to Robbie's surprise sent back e-mails explaining the assignments more fully than Robbie's modest reports on them. As a result, Robbie rebounded quite strongly and regained some of the pleasure he had felt for the course—and for Mr. H.

As I tutored Robbie, I needed to interpret his claims about Mr. Higginbotham as a problem for Robbie to solve. Robbie needed to learn to react to the difficulties of staying organized with the new habits and skills that I had helped him to acquire. If I had allowed him to continue his habit of becoming frustrated only, he would never have gained greater independence and confidence. If I'd involved myself with his teacher, it would have taken away from his sense that he could make the necessary adjustments and achieve this on his own. It would also have made it more difficult for Robbie to shift with such agility from enjoying Mr. H., to being upset with him, to enjoying him once again.

The (So-Called) Underutilized Teacher

Robbie had another problematic relationship with a teacher. For the first semester, his work in English class was mediocre. He was disengaged, and he spoke ill of Ms. Bogart, his teacher. Ms. Bogart was judgmental and tough. When the first quarter ended, Robbie received a grade that was well below his ability. He said he didn't care.

A week later, I received an e-mail from Ms. Bogart. She had contacted Robbie's mother, who had told her about me. Ms. Bogart asked if we could speak about Robbie. She thought he was underperforming and was a little turned off by her. He had missed two assignments, for which she had forgiven him (so much for Ms. Bogart's alleged "toughness"). Meanwhile, Robbie had shown raw ability on a creative writing assignment. She wondered if I could encourage Robbie to see her regularly about his creative work.

I didn't tell him about my contact with Ms. Bogart. Instead, I asked to see his creative writing assignments for the class, which Robbie had somehow forgotten to show me. In the most recent of them, Ms. Bogart praised

Robbie for the potential within it. She'd casually asked him to drop by.

I asked him if he'd done so.

"Are you kidding?" he said. "Where's the good in that?"

"Why do you think she wants to see you?" I asked.

"I've no idea," Robbie said. He added, "Probably just to tell me what I did wrong." There was no real conviction in his words.

"You don't believe that," I said to him.

So Robbie visited Ms. Bogart. He didn't report on it, but I received an e-mail from her a few weeks later, thanking me and informing me that Robbie had actually dropped in on her two additional times, both unannounced.

In a short time, Robbie's interest in English increased. His attitude toward Ms. Bogart changed, and he soon began to produce intelligent, above-average critical essays as well. His work in this class boosted his interest in English for the following year.

Ms. Bogart was underutilized by Robbie even if it was not apparent to Robbie. My role sometimes includes ensuring that the opportunities teachers provide aren't lost on the student. My contact was kept hidden from Robbie because I didn't want to intervene in his developing a productive relationship with a teacher. He needed to discover that he could do that and even change his mind about a teacher that he at first had scorned.

Whether in or out of contact with the teacher, the tutor develops the student's ability to learn regardless of the challenges of the circumstances. In some cases, the information the teacher supplies the tutor or the tutor provides the teacher advances this goal of intellectual independence. In other cases, the student is better off if the tutor remains out of contact. Case by case, based on the principle of intellectual independence, parents should expect the tutor to decide on what works best. The goal is as always to build your child's abilities and confidence, to end tutoring work with your child, and to return your child to the school.

As these last four chapters have demonstrated, this principle of *intellectual independence* determines the relationships tutors should cultivate with student, parent, and finally the teacher. That same principle applies in the role tutors play with more specialized cases of students with learning disabilities and emotional disorders, which are addressed in the next two chapters.

CHAPTER FIVE

The Challenges of Learning Disabilities

The previous chapters have focused on the general issues of tutoring, including who needs it; the proper approach to it; and the relationships between tutors, parents, students, and teachers. This is the first of two specialty chapters. It addresses students diagnosed with learning disabilities. It doesn't presume to tell parents how to tutor students for each specific disability. It focuses instead on the issues that learning disabilities raise for the tutoring of their children.

For a small but significant portion of the population of students, learning disabilities are a real and present part of their experience.

All students encounter learning difficulties of some kind. I've had brilliant students in history and English who are at a total loss in math; above-average students in science and math who are utterly flummoxed by a poem; and good students in most academic subjects who struggle to draw or to paint and couldn't navigate their way around a city or town if their lives depended on it.

And yet students diagnosed as learning disabled (LD) have been singled out, lumped together under this classification because their difficulties are more conspicuous within formal education and sometimes more severe. They may be as intelligent as anyone at their schools, but their intelligence or means of learning doesn't get a significant amount of appreciation within a school setting. Although some students' abilities enable them to perform well in schools, LD students have not done well in some or all subjects.

So they are diagnosed as LD, which in some school systems is like being removed to a different country, with its own special flag. In other cases, LD students are not so much taught as tolerated in the general classroom, where the needs of most students must rule.

What Does Learning Disabled Mean?

Before looking at the typical issues that parents should expect tutors to address, we need a short, clear description of who these students are. If we follow the definition in a landmark federal law, the Individuals with Disabilities Education Act of 1975 (IDEA), we find that learning disabilities are disorders that students have in the use or understanding of "spoken or written languages." These disorders appear in students as "an imperfect ability to listen, think, speak, read, write, spell or to do mathematical calculations."

The definition of LD within this law may seem clear, but what does "imperfect ability" mean? Who, after all, has perfect ability? Effectively, the law describes imperfect ability as when a student's academic achievement doesn't measure up to his or her intellectual potential.

It's only fair to say that there are competing definitions of learning disabilities. The controversies surround how to measure the difference between the achievement and the potential of a student, what level of difficulty describes a learning disability, and even how lasting such a disability is. For example, the National Institute of Neurological Disorders and Stroke declares that learning disabilities "can be" lifelong disorders: so much for certainty.

In categories familiar to parents, we can classify the most common learning disabilities in this way:

- Reading Disorder (Dyslexia)
- Arithmetic Disorder (Dyscalculia)
- Writing Disorder (Dysgraphia, Graphomotor Disorder)
- Disorder of Written Expression
- Language Disorder

(*Source:* Kennedy-Krieger Institute Web listing, kenne dykrieger.org/, bulleted in this way.)

Parents should note two important aspects of this definition. First, it doesn't include attention deficit hyperactivity disorder (ADHD), which is a group of behavioral disorders that are sometimes but not always associated with learning disabilities. Second, these students may be intelligent but are thwarted because of some kind of neurodevelopmental dysfunction.

LD students have pronounced learning difficulties, but their difficulties fall along a spectrum of inabilities that many if not all students have. In some cases, those difficulties remain severe throughout their lives; in other cases, they can be compensated for or simply not pose the problems they do in school. School often focuses on memorization, linguistic abilities, and assorted other aptitudes to a degree people don't experience in their work lives. Once working, LD students can flourish and can find their abilities and intelligence more readily recognized than in school.

There are countless examples of individuals who struggle in school but later come into their own. I know of a prominent literary scholar who suffers from dyslexia but has read widely and has written books that would humble nearly anyone. I know an accomplished individual with extraordinary social skills and rare talents for economic analysis who stopped reading books in grade school. (The last one was *Charlotte's Web*.)

In middle school and high school, however, these students were more lost than others; and yet their intelligence and abilities were there to be found. This does not mean the school is at fault. It means that the student's intelligence and abilities didn't map well onto the terrain of school.

LD students deserve their own chapter because they present issues for tutoring that are particular to them and because LD seems to be diagnosed more often in adolescence than at any other age. The Children's Data Bank reports that as of 2004, approximately 8 percent of the school-age population of the United States received diagnoses of learning disabilities. Among students between twelve and seventeen years old, that percentage increases significantly, to 10.5 percent (*Source:* Children's Data Bank, http://www.childtrendsdatabank.org/tables/65_Table_1.htm).

In short, the LD diagnosis is a real part of the experience of many adolescents.

The Role of Tutoring for Learning Disabled Students

Learning disabilities create additional complications for tutoring. For parents, those additional complications should have a big impact on whom they choose to tutor their child.

The overall goal of tutoring remains the same—
intellectual independence. And there is no single answer for
how to tutor LD students, just as there is no one-size-fits-
all style for any other kind of student. One LD student
may need help creating a set of learning habits that allow
her to go on with learning in or out of school; another
may need help pursuing his talents and interests; and
some students will need help with both. The focus of this
chapter is on what commonly enhances and what commonly inhibits the success of tutoring an LD student.

The chapter does not advise parents on how a tutor
should work with each specific kind of learning disability. Parents don't need a book to tell them that they
should find a tutor who is experienced or trained at working with the specific difficulty their child has, from dyslexia to dyscalculia. You don't need that any more than
you need someone to tell you that the tutor should know
organic chemistry, calculus, American history, or mod-
ernist poetry, if those are the subjects your child needs
help with.

In spite of all the differences, there are common issues
for tutoring LD students. In practical terms, parents can
see these problems through a consideration of two topics:
the challenges of LD for students and the challenges of
LD for parents.

Students have as many reactions to their learning
disabilities as there are personalities. And yet there are
typical reactions that parents should expect tutors to be
keenly aware of:

- Students who are in significant distress
- Students who aren't ready to make wholesale changes
- Students who are diverted from their interests by their
  difficulties

Students Who Are in Distress

Jeremy was overwhelmed. A second-semester freshman in high school, he had been diagnosed with severe dyscalculia and less severe language-processing problems. There was little doubt that Jeremy had pronounced difficulties in math. He needed extra help from his math teacher at least once a week. He often had to take math tests twice before he could eke out a passing grade. A multistepped problem in math was agony. Algebra and geometry were altogether out of reach for him. In science, he was constantly in danger of failing, largely because of his difficulty with computation, and his capacities for conceptualizing were also extremely weak.

I had been hired to shore him up as he went through high school, to make him more confident that he could learn, especially in English and history, where his circumstances were less dire than in math and science but where he struggled, too. I was also asked to "see what I could do" to help him through the elementary math course in which he was enrolled, supplementing his math teacher's in-school help.

Jeremy's parents were most worried about what all his struggles were doing to his sense of self. He was a sweet kid at home, but at school he sometimes got in trouble. In the first semester of his freshman year, Jeremy's math teacher had embarrassed him by forcing him to answer a question before the entire class.

After a short attempt, Jeremy had exploded. "Do the problem yourself, for shit's sake."

His outburst had earned him a one-day suspension from school. He managed to switch math classes in the second semester, in part because he received a D-minus for the first semester. But the threat of disciplinary problems remained, because Jeremy was constantly humiliated at school.

Jeremy's father was a mechanical engineer and his mother was a social worker. Their academic accomplishments made Jeremy's struggles all the worse. As sensitive and accepting of him as his parents were, he was constantly reminded of their difference from him. He frequently complained that they couldn't possibly imagine his experience. School had been easy for them.

I recall my brief forays into math with Jeremy. When we addressed an area of difficulty, he listened carefully to every word I said and executed practice problems with me. Once he would try a practice problem on his own, however, he was utterly lost. A blank expression came across his face. He stared at the page with no apparent sense of comprehension. After a while, he'd surrender. His lips would purse, and he'd rub the page of paper with his hands, as if trying to erase its contents.

I was careful in my reaction to him. In as neutral a way as possible, I would walk him through the problem in practice, step-by-step. When he could complete a step on his own, I'd note his accomplishment to him but without any exaggerated sense of celebration. He would nod his head at such moments, weakly hopeful. In the end, however, he remained soured by his inability.

One day toward the end of a session, I leaned back and stretched my arms. As I did so, the chair tilted back according to its normal capacities and then suddenly gave way. I got up quickly, thinking the chair was going to topple over.

Jeremy reached for the chair. "Let me see it," he said.

He inverted the chair and began looking at its mechanisms. His fingers traced the gears and rods gently, without trying to turn anything. "I'll bring some tools next time," he said. I decided at that moment not to repair the chair myself but to wait on Jeremy.

At our next session, he showed up with a set of screwdrivers and a wrench. He turned the chair over again, but this time he went to work. Fifteen minutes later, he had fixed the chair.

"How did you do that?" I asked him.

"I don't know," he said. "I just did." He smiled.

Jeremy's success gave me an idea. Although his high school had no courses in shop or industrial arts, it did have an active drama program. And putting on plays requires building sets. The next week, I asked Jeremy if he had any interest in working behind the scenes of a play.

"Doing what?" he said.

"I don't know," I told him. "I'm sure they have more than chairs that need fixing."

Jeremy didn't reject the suggestion. A week later, he reported that he had started to help out with a production of *Our Town*. Within another few weeks, he began explaining to me the various problems with the technical staging of the production and the creation of sets. As he described his work behind the scenes, he couldn't help but express genuine interest and satisfaction.

The semester went on; Jeremy's struggles in math and science continued. He showed modest progress in English and history. Although his work remained below average, Jeremy was nonetheless changing. He was less affected by his struggles in these courses. He took them in stride. His parent's worried less about his behavior at school.

The following year, Jeremy was a virtual impresario of technical matters in the drama department. Lighting, scenery, and sets—he was soon the expert among all the students, commanding a crew of backstage workers. In his classes, Jeremy managed to tolerate what was going on. In the theater, he was a man on fire, the go-to guy, the one who took responsibility.

As Jeremy neared his senior year, his high school guidance counselor worried to his parents about his academic record. Where would Jeremy go to college? Fortunately, Jeremy's parents took the guidance counselor's concerns in stride. They told the guidance counselor that Jeremy would find some school or situation to accept him for who he was and what he wanted to do.

The next year, Jeremy went to one of the city colleges in New York. I stayed in touch with him. He reported there were many students "like me" at his college. "I don't like it much," he told me, "but I don't feel like such a freak. And I don't have to take any more math."

Meanwhile, he had taken some technical courses in the drama department and had begun work on a college theater production. He also started volunteering at an off, off-Broadway theater. "I'm thinking I should do something like get a union card if I'm going to do anything more with this," he said. "Maybe I'll have to do an apprenticeship program, but that might be better than college anyway. I may look into film work, too."

The greatest help I provided Jeremy with probably came from waiting for him to fix my chair. This helped him gain respect for his mechanical ability. It was something he could do for which the school had not yet recognized him.

Assessing Jeremy's Story. Throughout my tutoring of Jeremy, his biggest problem didn't come from his inabilities in math and science. It was his attitude toward his inabilities. Jeremy's difficulties were of two kinds: not appreciating his abilities and intelligence for what they were and wrestling with the reality that he had a harder time than most other students in his high school classes.

His story reflects his difficulties with accepting how he thought and developed. Fueled by his expectations that he should be like his parents, dispirited by his diagnosis as LD, Jeremy needed to discover a way to prize the abilities and intelligence he had.

Working with LD students requires a tutor to be alert to their repeated doubts of their own intelligence. In Jeremy's case, he needed to accept how he learned, where he flourished, and how to appreciate the kind of intelligence that he had.

Tutoring helped by turning him away from his distress and toward his abilities. In Jeremy's case, intellectual independence meant valuing the learning and development that he experienced outside of academic subjects, where he was truly inspired.

Students Who Aren't Ready to Make Wholesale Changes

Whereas Jeremy experienced frustration and distress, Mark gave up. A talented student in science and mathematics, especially with computers, Mark had conspicuous dyslexia and language disorders, complicated by attention deficit disorder.

If Mark tried to read an especially long sentence, he could not take in its full meaning from beginning to end without several attempts. He rarely tried, preferring instead to skip along the surface, grasping at the occasional meaning of a single word. Then he would move on to the next sentence and the next in similar fashion. If the prose told a story and was heavily plotted, he could sometimes explain what happened. If it was a definition of an idea, the analysis of a historical event, or anything that did not lend itself to quick apprehension, he couldn't follow it.

Mark's parents were alert, careful, and patient with him, but Mark was impatient with his difficulties and uninterested in doing much about them. His parents hired a first-rate tutor to work with him. Mark dutifully attended sessions for a while, but he eventually gave up.

"It's not going to work," he told his parents.

As a result, he rarely understood what he read unless it was discussed in class. In fact, what he really understood was class discussion of the reading. And his essays were often disorganized and superficial, as well as filled with sentence fragments and punctuation errors.

From class discussion, his teachers noted his capacity for insight. At his school, this was enough to keep his record from declining. So he was a steady, average performer throughout his high school career.

Mark graduated and went off to a technology-oriented college, where he encountered immediate trouble passing its writing requirements. He came home frustrated but determined for the first time to get at his problems. He enrolled in a summer course on essay writing to complete his requirements, and he came to me to help him address the obstacles to his progress.

Mark struggled mightily to comprehend what he read and wrote for that course. I began by insisting that he read and reread all of the required reading of the course— which was a selection of essays—sentence by sentence. I asked him to take notes that focused on identifying the most salient points in each paragraph and relating it to the thesis of the essay. I had him outline his reading of an essay and even diagram the relationship between the topic sentence and the other sentences within a paragraph.

Slowly, he read with greater understanding but often imperfectly, missing key ideas. His writing, however, benefited from this approach. He liked the diagramming of paragraphs and outlining of ideas. For his second essay for the course, he developed a detailed outline that was nearly a first draft. Throughout the course, he struggled to produce fluidity in his essays, but they all had discernible arguments. He passed the course and returned to college.

My work with Mark did not produce a great change in him, but it initiated something. During the first semester of his sophomore year, he occasionally contacted me as a deadline for a paper came due, asking me to read through his drafts. He still struggled with fluidity, and he had to be reminded to create a well-organized outline. "Oh, yeah," he would joke, "I remember that."

Then he stopped contacting me. At the end of the spring semester, I called him to see how he was doing. He had completed all of his essays for an anthropology course on time and received above-average grades on them. He sent me copies of them. They were substantial improvements on any work he'd done while I had tutored him.

Mark was willful, and I was lucky with him. If I had been his first tutor a year or two earlier, I doubt I would have had much success. What made all the difference was that he finally reached the point where he felt he needed to improve. He was ready to address the problem, and he discovered he was able to. I suspect that writing and reading will never come easily for him. I'm sure, however, it is far easier now.

Mark's case is a lesson in the potential for real improvement where a student is challenged by a substantial difficulty. The improvement may be far more modest with other students, but so much depends on their motivation, their willingness to work hard, and their ability to settle on a reasonable expectation. When Mark was ready, he made progress.

Students Who Are Diverted from Their Interests by Their Difficulties

In still other cases, the learning disability becomes an obsession, a source of frustration on which the student fixes, distracting him from what might otherwise interest him. There was something of that in the case of Jeremy. There was more of that in the story of Louis. Once Louis accepted his limitations, it allowed him to discover a genuine passion.

Louis was a fourteen-year-old freshman whose language-processing disorder strongly affected his reading comprehension and writing. He was an outgoing kid, who shifted between being angry at himself for his below-average performance in English and being certain that he could be a really great writer someday. He truly didn't seem to have any interest in writing. He rarely liked to read and wouldn't write much on his own. It's just that when he had a school English assignment, he would declare, "I should be able to do this a whole lot better. I can do this a whole lot better."

For more than a year, while he slowly improved, he frustrated himself with expectations that were always well out of reach. Eventually, he admitted he was doing this. He did not stop working to improve in reading and writing, but he grew easier on himself.

Within a few months, he discovered a new interest: creating films. Here was something that came easily to him. He liked it. He threw all of himself into it. Within a year, he had created a series of short films that brought him considerable recognition within his school. When he graduated, he entered à school of the arts with a sophisticated film program.

Once Louis recognized that his expectations had been unrealistic, he was freed to look at what genuinely interested him. He'd been caught up in his struggle to overcome all elements of his learning difficulty—as if it could somehow be totally eliminated from him. That obsessive focus had eclipsed much of his capacity to explore other interests and abilities he might have. When he wasn't caught up anymore, it was as if he were returning from the dark side of the moon. He found a bright, new world to investigate, which led him to film.

There are of course students who are LD who need no such special reminder to focus on their interests and accept their abilities for what they are. Carol was a high school student with a distinct interest in history and social science and pronounced dyscalculia. In English and history, she had exceptional analytical and conceptual abilities. She wrote superior essays for both subjects. Carol made her way through high school, a happy student who struggled with math. Eventually, she was accepted into a fine college, excelled in English, and went on to pursue a career as a writer and editor.

These cases describe a variety of responses to learning disabilities that parents should expect tutors to understand and to respond to with something akin to mental agility. Tutors should recognize where a student attacks himself for his difficulties and be resourceful enough to find ways to honor the student's strengths; they should be alert to the possibilities that students will perceive themselves as unintelligent; they should be watchful for when a student is not ready to work intently at lessening the effect of a disability; and they should be canny enough to see where the drama of coping with a disability masks the student's capacity to discover true interests.

The Challenges of Learning Disabilities for Parents

Jeremy, Mark, and Louis showed that students with learning disabilities can be their own worst enemy. In other cases, it can be the parent who presents the problem.

Lillian was a sixteen-year-old sophomore in high school, the daughter of the executive director of a non-profit organization and a college English professor. She was severely dyslexic, but she insisted that she loved to read even if it took her much longer to do it than most students at her school.

Unfortunately, her speed at reading caused her great difficulty once she entered high school. Over the course of the last two years, as the demands within each subject increased, Lillian's grades dropped precipitously.

Lillian's father comforted her repeatedly. He insisted that it did not matter how she did in school so long as she tried and took pleasure from it. Her mother, the English professor, had a harder time accepting Lillian's condition. Her mother had read "virtually everything written on dyslexia," from books on the approach of learning specialists to statistics on the reading comprehension of dyslexics.

Lillian's mother held out the hope that with hard work, Lillian would soon grow out of her reading difficulties. She pointed to Lillian's apparent success during a short poetry unit in English as a sign of her daughter's potential.

Beginning in grade school, Lillian had seen numerous learning specialists. She had had early intervention to improve her reading, using the Orton Gillingham approach. She had had intensive, one-on-one instruction and learned guided oral reading. These various specialists had made Lillian a more accurate and fluent reader, but their success had its limits. Now Lillian's parents had moved past specialists in dyslexia to me.

In the past year, Lillian, a sweet but passionate adolescent, had become increasingly upset about her lack of progress. Even her work in courses that did not require much reading took a dip, as the school year continued, which her parents attributed to her distress. She was willing to see me because she wanted this overall decline in her performance to stop.

Lillian made an immediate impression. She arrived dressed in a dark blue jacket that had a collar made of small beads strung in rows, about three fingers thick. The beads gave the appearance of alternating bands of color across her neck—white, blue, and red—like a porcupine-quill necklace. She had made the collar herself, she told me, and had even done some work tailoring the jacket.

I asked if I could see her coursework and notebooks. She laid a series of well-organized, immaculate notebooks on the desk, each of them listing her homework assignments in letters that bordered on calligraphy. From the notes she took during our session, it was apparent that she could print letters like that as easily as most people could write script.

I told Lillian that I was impressed by her handwriting. Pointing at the collar of her jacket, I told her she was clearly gifted. She beamed.

Then I asked her what she thought she needed help with. She hesitated a moment and then answered. "When I'm in a good mood, I'd say there is no problem. I'm just not that good at reading and writing. But a lot of the time, I get into a bad mood and think I just can't do what I should be doing."

I asked her what puts her in a good mood: "Drawing," she said instantly, "and making clothes."

We decided on a routine where she would meet reading deadlines for each of our meetings. Then she would reread and be drilled for comprehension during the tutoring session. I would read everything she was assigned so I could ensure that she was understanding the most fundamental elements of her assigned reading and if possible the nuances. She would adjust any notes she took for reading after the session and then use those for the basis of writing assignments as they arose.

I reported on our first meeting to Lillian's parents. When I mentioned her clothes and handwriting to her parents, her father spoke in glowing terms about her abilities in art and described her room as though it were a museum piece.

Lillian's mother was impatient with all this talk. "It's nice of you to notice," she told me, "but it isn't why we hired you."

Within a few weeks, I was convinced that Lillian was one of the most organized and hardest-working students I had ever encountered. I also believed that she was working at her limits in reading, at least for now. And I continued to be impressed by the clothing designs and illustrations that she brought in to show me on occasion, just for fun.

At our next session, I told her that I could continue to help her improve her reading, but I thought she was working exactly as she should on her own. More important, I told her that she was doing just fine. Lillian began to cry. "I think I knew I was," she said.

I arranged a telephone conversation with both parents to report my conclusions: the tutoring sessions had slightly improved Lillian's understanding of her assigned reading because they provided intense, individualized discussions for her; but I was relatively certain that Lillian was working to her capacity, at least for now. Lillian's mother was not happy to hear it.

"She can develop more with time and effort," she said. "I know the literature says that dyslexics will always find it hard to read, but she's getting better. Her reading comprehension is already pretty good."

"That may be," I said. "I think you're more expert than I am on what she might eventually be able to do. But for now, she seems to be doing all that she can. She's having trouble accepting that." Gently, I added, "She may think she's disappointing you."

I remember thinking at the time that the parents had a choice: Lillian could be appreciated for her abilities now, including her impressive abilities in art and design; or she could be repeatedly pushed to do more than she was able to do at present as a reader. If they took the second course, things at school were likely to get worse in all her subjects. Lillian's parents were intelligent, caring people. They didn't need me to say that.

Sure enough, a few days later, Lillian's mother sent me a simple e-mail: "I think you're right for now."

I was pleased to hear this. Something had shifted within the family, so that her mother appeared to be more accepting. Lillian's mother asked that I continue to work with Lillian for the remainder of the school year, exercising her ability to read with depth and accuracy. But I shouldn't push her or give her the impression that she had to do better.

I wanted to make sure that Lillian got the right message from me, so each session, I began by asking her about art and fashion. She loved to talk about clothing, and she brought in samples of her work and books of art that she admired. Soon enough, a small but significant portion of the sessions was taken up with everyone from Rothko to the color field artists to Monet.

As she shared her interests, Lillian grew progressively more relaxed during her visits to me and less upset about her history and English courses. Her performance improved in her nonreading courses. In history and English, she continued to decline but then leveled off. She did not show any of the signs of distress from earlier in the year. She went on to attend the Fashion Institute of Technology in New York, presumably to have a career in fashion design or illustration.

Assessing Lillian's Story. The more I listened to Lillian and her parents, the more I realized that the best way I could help her was to establish distinctly different goals for her tutoring sessions than those her mother had wanted initially. If I'd challenged her to read still better, I would have done harm. She was already pedaling as fast as she could.

Starting each session with a discussion of art, design, and clothing was a way of recognizing her abilities and helping her to accept what she could do in reading. Until then, her dyslexia had become not simply a cause of reading difficulties but a drag on her confidence in her ability in other subjects. I tried to counter that effect by first acknowledging her talents with clothes and design work and then moving on to reading.

Whatever efforts I made, however, had a modest effect when compared with the effect of Lillian's mother. She had had a difficult time accepting Lillian's limitations as a reader. In time, she recognized that when she challenged her daughter to read better, it seemed to Lillian as if her mother refused to accept what Lillian could do at any given moment. She would probably never be as good a reader as she would an artist. Eventually her mother had recognized this and became one of her daughter's strongest supporters for her work in fashion and design.

With LD students, tutors should be alert for students and parents who have difficulty focusing on where the student's abilities and interests lie. Parents should expect tutors to advocate for realism and patience: realism about what an LD student can and cannot do at any given time and patience for what the LD student may be able to do, because research has shown that some disabilities can be outgrown or compensated for over time. In some cases, that will mean tutors will disagree with the focus that parents believe the tutor should take. Tutors aren't infallible, but parents should want this kind of independence in the tutor they hire to work with their child.

This chapter asks parents to remember that the tutor works directly and indirectly with LD students for the following reasons:

- To teach skills and learning habits for meeting their specific challenges
- To focus on the process of learning
- To help them identify interests and abilities
- To appreciate how they learn as a potential asset
- To steer them forever away from the notion that a learning disability equates with a lack of intelligence
- To avoid viewing their disability as a pathology

Tutors should help focus LD students and parents alike on recognizing that there is no single path to learning and accomplishment. The tutor should counsel for realism and patience, for what the student is able or willing to do now. He should accept the student's performance as it is and avoid predicting how much the student will be able to overcome or compensate for the disability in the future. In all these ways, the tutor attempts to create a sense of confidence in the abilities and interests of the student. The experience of learning for the LD student is both like and utterly different from other students. The goal of tutoring is to make that difference utterly comfortable and promising to the student.

The next chapter focuses on another population of students for whom the experience of learning and tutoring presents unique challenges: students with psychological difficulties.

CHAPTER SIX

The Challenges of Psychological Difficulties

This second specialty chapter addresses students with distinct, psychological difficulties that affect their abilities in school. Tutors can help these students develop intellectual independence by structuring and otherwise supporting their academic work as they are treated by therapists.

Serena, a second-semester senior in college, had repeatedly failed courses. She had been trying to complete her college education for seven years, at four different educational institutions. In high school, she had received a vague diagnosis of a language-processing disorder, but her high school provided minimal support services. It also inflated her grades so that she passed through school without her difficulties receiving much attention. She had received tutoring back then, but it had covered up her problems because the tutor and her parents effectively did her schoolwork for her.

Now Serena's psychiatrist had referred her to me. He told me that Serena suffered from manic depression and a substance abuse problem, but she was stabilized on medication. She had concentration problems, which the psychiatrist believed had three potential sources: her medication for depression, the occasional marijuana she used, and the volatile family life she had because she lived at home with her parents.

A First Impression

When I met Serena, I was struck by how articulate and bright she was. She was fluent in four languages and had the capacity to lock on to a conversation and listen with genuine intelligence.

And yet around schoolwork, Serena was insecure and openly nervous. She struggled to write even the simplest of paragraphs. She could not maintain a line of thought through the length of an essay. In spite of her difficulties, she was committed to completing her college degree that semester. She had only a writing course and an urban studies course to finish. Still, her psychiatrist was concerned she would once again sabotage herself and fail.

Creating a Structure

Given the difficulties that Serena faced, I knew that I would have to provide a highly structured approach to ease her insecurities, and I would have to hold her to strict deadlines to prevent the workload from overwhelming her.

Serena was reasonably comfortable with reading, so I focused our efforts on her writing assignments. In a planner, we entered the due dates for written work in both of her courses. Next I walked her through a process of writing that included well-defined stages, each with deadlines: collecting notes, assessing ideas, building an outline and paragraphs, writing a draft, and revising it. I told her that we would work on each stage as if it were a distinct task and set the worries about completing the entire essay aside. If she focused only on the task at hand, she'd eventually get the essay done.

Working back from the deadline for her papers, we placed due dates for each stage into the planner. (As the semester continued, we also placed the dates of tests in the planner and once again worked back from those dates to establish when she should begin studying for them. But Serena had little trouble preparing for or taking exams.)

Overcoming Insecurities

Serena's approach to the first stage of her first paper was revealing. She had to write an essay on *The Death and Life of Great American Cities,* by Jane Jacobs, but she had not taken notes or written down her thoughts while reading or during class lectures on the book. Her difficulties had qualified her for note-taking aides during class, so that she could concentrate on what was being said. I wasn't convinced that these aides were entirely good for her. I thought it was likely that she was a visually oriented learner and needed to see her thoughts in writing to remember them or develop them.

I tested out that possibility as she began to collect ideas for her reading of the book. Serena was uncertain that she had any thoughts at all while they remained simply in her mind. I offered to act temporarily as a scribe, writing down her ideas as she spoke them. She managed to make a few observations; I wrote them down. The appearance of her ideas on the page had an immediate effect. As soon as she saw the notes on the paper, she took the pen from me and began to write down more ideas.

Serena was in the end satisfied and even happy with the note-taking stage of writing the essay. Yet when she started on the next stage, organizing her ideas, a similar anxiety arose: Could she do this? The net gain of accomplishing the first stage was washed away in a wave of insecurity. Her reaction turned out to be part of a distinct pattern that related to her concentration problems. Each task, no matter how small, took her time to understand. It was as if she were viewing the task through a lens that only slowly came into focus. First, she showed confusion. She expressed doubt that she understood. Next, she showed a tentative understanding. Finally, she completed the stage.

I pointed out this pattern to her, telling her to anticipate that this would happen with each stage. It didn't bring her much satisfaction.

"I don't think that will ever change," she complained.

When the essay was finished, however, she commented that "Writing was different this time." Whether she considered this to be a good difference was unclear from her tone, but I took it as a reason for optimism.

Serena completed the next essay with a little more ease, although she was still tentative. She had to be reminded what to do at each stage of the writing process. During the third essay, she was more baffled that she was able to do the work than she was confused.

The Surprise of Success

As the semester neared its end, her anxieties increased and her confidence, fragile to begin with, wavered. I doubled the number of tutoring sessions per week and divided up each day into blocks of time. For each of those blocks, I established goals for completing work. I also asked her to check in with me via e-mail every couple of days.

I gently reminded her of her recent successes, too. I told her that she now had a way of getting her papers done. When she had begun working this way, she had little faith that it would help. Now she had a proven record. She should remember that in spite of her doubts, there was a good chance that taking things stage by stage would work once again.

During the final two weeks of the semester, Serena dutifully checked in with me. She was productive and turned papers in on time. As she worked on the final paper of her college career, she said to me with surprise, "I'm going to get this done."

When I last saw Serena, she was grateful yet stunned that college was over for her.

"I was so used to doing it I didn't think it would ever end."

Her psychiatrist reported that Serena showed a genuine boost in her confidence as well as relief. "It's an accomplishment that she can't help but notice," the psychiatrist said.

Help for Students with Psychological Difficulties

Serena's story is one example of a limited but truly important role that a tutor can play with students who have psychological difficulties. While a therapist addresses the student's emotional difficulties and provides counsel to the tutor, the tutor can help provide stability for the student's academic life, which increases her chances of success.

Serena was bright enough to complete the work on her own, but her psychological difficulties had complicated her ability to work. They had undermined her confidence and blocked her from realizing she had the ability. They had prevented her from developing the study habits that would ensure she could get the work done.

In response, tutoring provided a kind of cognitive support. It steered around her serious emotional issues, of course—those were for the psychiatrist to address—while it coached her to work in a way that minimized her anxiety. It contributed to her sense of achievement by helping her slowly and steadily to build a record of accomplishment with each essay completed.

Structuring a Student's Academic Life

Serena gained academic stability because tutoring provided additional structure to her life as a student. The confusions and turbulence of her emotional life made the challenges of learning more chaotic for her. The weekly tutoring sessions were one kind of structure. Tutoring sessions provided a way of organizing her experience of learning, because they were weekly and because they increased as her needs did toward the end of the semester. Serena was calmer than in the past, she said, because she knew she could address her academic concerns in tutoring.

The instructions I gave Serena on how to write essays were also an important structure for her. Dividing up her time into note taking, organizing, and writing allowed her to combat the insecurities she experienced when writing. The stages for writing with clear deadlines made the confusion more tolerable and helped to prevent her anxiety about writing from overwhelming her.

Similarities and Differences

Looking back through the other chapters, you will see that there is nothing especially new or startlingly different about the methods of tutoring Serena from those used tutoring any other student. Other students needed well-planned approaches to completing all assignments and taking exams. Other students needed methodical ways of writing essays or extra help during crunch time. Other students suffered from confusion, lack of confidence, and anxieties about completing their work.

Tutoring students with psychological difficulties often calls for the same repertoire of tutoring styles that it does with all other students. It requires a tutor to listen well, to observe carefully, and to decide which particular techniques fit best for the student.

Just as important, the goal of tutoring students with psychological difficulties is the same as it is for all students: to provide students with intellectual independence; to teach students how they learn and to provide habits that allow them to work well on their own.

Serena recognized, however tentatively, that she had found a way of approaching each paper that would last far beyond her experience with me.

Yet there are essential differences in working with a student with psychological difficulties:

- The student needs emotional stability.
- Things aren't always as they seem.

The Student Needs Emotional Stability

Sustaining emotional stability in students with chronic or acute psychological problems requires the individual to be in treatment with a therapist. It is also essential for the tutoring to be effective. My work with Serena would not have been successful if she hadn't been carefully monitored by her therapist and on medication. And though there may be exceptions, students with psychological difficulties usually want therapeutic support or discover they need it soon enough.

For example, a psychologist referred to me a sixteen-year-old student whom she had diagnosed with a mood disorder when he had been brought to her because of learning difficulties. Eli's parents were convinced that their son would never go to therapy willingly, and they were uncertain that therapy was really what he needed.

The therapist recommended that I try to work with Eli on the slim chance the parents were right, that therapy wasn't necessary. If tutoring didn't work, the therapist reasoned to me, it might convince the parents to seek psychological help. I was reluctant, but the therapist promised to advise me. After a month and a half of constant struggles, in which the student grew increasingly upset at any gesture I made to scrutinize his work, Eli's parents met with me. It turned out their son was the same way at school whenever a teacher tried to address him individually.

Eli's parents seemed to get the message. Their son needed a therapist to stabilize him before he would be available for tutoring—or most learning at school, for that matter. It took time before that therapy was successful, but eventually it made the student ready to be tutored. Eli needed a fresh start, with a new tutor, but he did beautifully and is now working without any need for help. The lesson learned was that the stability of therapy was essential to the progress of the student in tutoring.

Things Aren't Always As They Seem

In many cases, the insights of the therapist are essential for tutoring to succeed. With any student, it takes a considerable amount of time to understand what they mean when they speak and how best to help them. Students with psychological difficulties are often much harder to understand for someone who has no clinical experience. Although tutors shouldn't ignore their instincts or perceptions about a student, a therapist is better trained at understanding a student in such conditions. The therapist is more likely to know what is most undermining of the student in emotional terms and what styles of communicating are most effective. Tutors should leverage whatever knowledge they can gain from the therapist to ensure they are productive with the student.

For example, a clinical psychologist referred to me a bright, earnest seventeen-year-old student with anxiety disorders. In my first session working with Alice, she had a test to prepare for in her American history course. I looked over Alice's plan for studying. I made a suggestion that she might spend a little more time on a few documents they had read, but otherwise I found her to have a good study plan. I told her that she could contact me if she had trouble sticking to it. Alice thanked me profusely for all of my help before we ended the session—far more thanks than the amount of help I gave her merited.

When I saw her next, I discovered that she had done a lot more than follow this study plan, which called for about eight hours of study spread over four days. She had worked for nearly thirty hours over those days, sacrificing almost all sleep. This was early in the game; her psychologist and I had not spoken at length. When we did speak, the psychologist was clear: Alice was panicked at changing her habits. She was looking for my approval to do exactly what she had been doing all along, act compulsively. I should try not to give her that approval.

"The good news is that Alice appears to be listening to what you say and taking it to heart," she told me.

"So tell her what she should do and what she shouldn't do. Set limits. I'll help her with her emotional reactions to this."

From then on, I tried to devise study habits for Alice that helped her to achieve competency with a subject but avoided her tendency to work obsessively until exhaustion. That included setting limits to the amount of time she should study for a given test or quiz, asking her to outline study material, restricting the number of examples she included in the outline with each idea, and placing strict time constraints on the drafting and revisions of essays. Eventually, Alice reduced her anxieties around schoolwork a great deal.

The therapist accelerated my ability to work with this student and prevented me from reinforcing the student's destructive tendencies.

In yet another example, the work of tutoring would have been impossible if not harmful without the help of the therapist. I had a very bright, seventeen-year-old student with depression and some aspects of borderline personality disorder, as her adolescent psychiatrist informed me. For more than a year and a half, Alexandra showed intermittent success followed by larger failure: a paper in history was excellent, but she flunked the entire course. She would see immediate improvement from coming to her sessions with me, but then she would disappear for weeks. By *my* standards, my work with her had largely failed.

But the problem was with my standards. As her psychiatrist pointed out, her borderline tendencies meant she would have trouble building a consistent relationship with me. The psychiatrist wondered if my expectations for the student had influenced her tendency to be out of contact with me.

The therapist was right. Once I learned not to expect consistent contact with the student, I changed goals in ways that helped her more. Alexandra was constantly playing catch-up in every course, the threat of failure or dismissal always before her. In the past, I had created a detailed schedule for her to complete all backup work. She always failed to meet that schedule. Now, with the therapist's insights, I made adjustments. I did away with the schedule altogether and established only small, immediate deadlines, for one day or perhaps two at most.

Focused in this way, Alexandra was more successful at chipping away at the backlog of work. She appeared for tutoring sessions more often. And though she still failed courses in the next semester, she created stronger work habits that made it possible for her to pass in the future.

Change for this student was glacially slow by some people's standards. Those people's standards didn't matter here nor did my standards. What mattered was how this student made changes. The therapist taught me what was realistic in this student's case.

Variations on Help for Students with Psychological Difficulties

So far in this chapter, we've outlined how tutoring can help students with psychological difficulties by providing a kind of academic stability and structure. But there are important variations in the kinds of assistance tutoring can provide students with psychological difficulties. Stated as general categories, they include

- Maintaining connection to school
- Adjusting to episodic difficulties

Maintaining Connection to School

Paula was an energetic twenty-one-year-old student with a passionate, extracurricular interest in politics, especially those centered on AIDS policy and social welfare. But for the past two years, she had been in academic limbo, and her political activity had been intermittent at best. Diagnosed with recurrent depression, her difficulties led her to go on medical leave from her university. She had taken most of the courses she needed to graduate, but she had nine incompletes that she needed to finish.

There was good reason for her medical leave. She had become unstable and was feeling better only in the past three months—just prior to her referral to me. As a result of the past few years, she had difficulty establishing a routine for getting work done, and she had lost confidence in her ability to be productive. Most important, she had lost her feeling of connection to the school itself overall.

"I know I'm smart," she said. "But I really don't ever remember being able to work on my own. Getting all these incompletes done—it's just overwhelming."

"She needs someone to follow her along as she works," her therapist told me. "She needs someone to establish a schedule for her and to show her that she can get the work done—to reconnect her to the school."

We began work on the first incomplete, an African history course for which Paula owed only a final, twenty-page paper. To start off, I had her write an e-mail to her professor, reminding him of her circumstances and declaring that she was going to complete this essay. The professor wrote back a welcoming note. This alone made Paula more dedicated to finishing the essay. She was nonetheless still nervous about whether she actually could complete it.

It helped that Paula had kept scrupulous research and class notes for that paper—as she had done for virtually all of her interrupted studies. Those notes made her work on the paper far easier than if she were starting from scratch. It meant that what she most needed was a way of reengaging herself in the work that she had already started, no matter how distant her memory of her efforts.

My first assignment for Paula was merely to read through her notes and assemble her ideas from them. She struggled with this assignment. She lost contact with me, only to return to tutoring a week and a half later, embarrassed by her absence. I welcomed her back and lightly dismissed her embarrassment as unnecessary. I told her I'd given her too hard an assignment to start out.

Then I began to review her notes with her. We talked about what ideas she had within the notes. As we did, she grew far more enlivened about the work. Noting this, I told her that she should go home and write a memo of the various ideas she'd had during our discussion. She wrote the memo. It in turn ignited her abilities. She finished going through the rest of her notes within another day.

We were now ready for her to write an outline. I gave her a few suggestions. Once again, she disappeared for a week and then returned without any of the outline done. I remember how she was energized by discussion, so I talked with her about what the outline should include and in what order. This time, she proposed that she should go home and write out a partial outline based on what we had discussed. She returned with a completed outline.

Each stage of work on Paula's first incomplete had a similar pattern: an initial assignment, a period of difficulty that led to her temporary disappearance, a return to work, and a bit of success. Eventually, in what took several more weeks than anticipated, Paula completed the paper and received credit for the course. In fact, she did well, an A-minus.

The success of the first reconnection fueled Paula's dedication. She completed a second incomplete and a third. In both cases, she continued to disappear when she had difficulty, but the length of time of her disappearance reduced with each incomplete she finished. I'm sure the therapist was a big help here, too. She had made considerable inroads with Paula, enabling her to function much better. Meanwhile, Paula began to volunteer once again for political organizations and even participated in an electoral campaign.

For each incomplete, I told Paula to recontact her professor to start off her work. Once she could see her pattern of success, she contacted more than one professor at a time. She was more confident that she would indeed get the work done.

Within a year, Paula had received credit for all of her incompletes and was ready to go off medical leave. She had one more course to complete her college degree. When papers came due for that course, Latin American history, Paula contacted me to ask for my help. She needed very little assistance, only reassurance that she was on target. In effect, she used my presence via tutoring sessions and e-mail as a way of keeping herself on track during each phase of work. She turned in all papers for that course on time and then graduated and went on to paid work in electoral politics.

A Transition for the Student

I helped Paula to reconnect with school, which meant returning to contact with professors, restoring her confidence in her intellect, and rebuilding her study habits.

In general, the tutor can function as this kind of transitional figure for the student, an intellectual liaison for her as she reexperiences and reconnects with school. All of this occurs as the tutor coaches the student to become increasingly more able and independent at pursuing her work.

Of course, the tutor can also help the student to maintain and build that connection with school in cases where the student is still in school. I had another student who experienced mild depression, causing him to take an incomplete, which he then finished over the summer. Anthony had a crisis of confidence when this occurred. He needed me to follow him through the next semester, reviewing his study habits and suggesting corrections.

Anthony was able enough to do the work. Although I made suggestions that improved his ability, my primary influence was to remind him of what he already knew how to do. The short, limited form of tutoring that Anthony required is an example of a tutor helping a student to make the change toward independence.

Adjusting to Episodic Difficulties

Tutors can also help students with psychological problems reconnect to school when some life event affects their ability to study and to produce work. You may recall the case of Alex in Chapter Three, a student paralyzed by his parents' divorce. He would have benefited from tutoring if the parents had been more communicative. Here is a comparable case that illustrates how tutoring can help.

Brett was a nineteen-year-old freshman in college referred to me by his therapist, who was concerned about Brett's poor performance. The therapist gave me a short history of Brett. He was raised in an upper-middle-class professional family, attended a good public school, and graduated in the top 10 percent of his class. He was a star swimmer who quit the team during his senior year of high school and then saw his grades slip during his final semester. His parents were enthusiastic that he had developed an interest in environmental concerns during the end of high school; but something seemed wrong, as he didn't follow through on any of these projects.

Brett arrived in college eager for the new experience. The initial reports were that he was attending all classes but having some difficulty staying on top of his work. (In retrospect, his therapist was uncertain that these first results were significant. She believed Brett might have "depressive tendencies," but she thought his first-semester performance might simply be the signs of someone adjusting to a new environment.)

Toward the middle of the first semester, Brett learned that his parents were divorcing, at which time his parents recommended that Brett seek counseling. In further conversations with Brett's psychologist, I learned that he was having difficulty handling the divorce. He was distracted and anxious. His prior psychological problems were exacerbated. He continued to attend all classes, although he was struggling to do above-average work. The therapist referred Brett to me so that I could evaluate his learning difficulties and help him get back on track, while the therapist dealt with his mood instability and emotional conflicts.

"I Used to Be Better at This"

When I met Brett, he was embarrassed to have sought me out, his pride wounded because he had always thought of himself as a very good student. I found that he had difficulty concentrating when writing or reading. He had problems synthesizing his various ideas into a cohesive whole, and he would complain, "I used to be better at this."

When I asked Brett what he did in high school to perform so well, he couldn't tell me. There was some evidence that he had simply gotten by on his considerable intellectual gifts. He said that he'd never taken notes and that he'd consistently done well in every class. And yet there was a second, altogether different reason for Brett's success: he thrived in high school because he maintained a structured study schedule. His parents were a large reason for that. They had encouraged him to work regularly every evening, sometimes scrutinizing what he produced.

These details made me think I needed to pursue two tracks with Brett: on the one hand, testing out what styles of learning worked best for him and creating a set of habits for him that fit with those styles; on the other hand, helping him to see that he could create a structured study schedule for himself. I ran this plan by his therapist before implementing it.

The therapist thought it would be helpful but pointed out that when it came to Brett trying to structure his studying, he would most likely feel some despair. It was exactly what his parents had done for him.

"So far as the scheduling is concerned, you may need to be more active," the therapist commented. "He'll probably need that at first."

Brett was dutiful about coming to tutoring sessions and seemed to welcome the time there. He was mostly relaxed and comfortable as he worked, but he would become markedly distressed when he found that he'd forgotten ideas he had while reading or lost track of his thoughts during class discussion. During a session, he occasionally threw his hands up in the air and shook his head in disbelief.

I suggested that he try to write down the essentials of his thoughts during class and then speak. I also told him that it wasn't unusual to find one's mind drifting during a complex conversation, especially during the first year of college. He believed he lost thoughts he had while reading; I told him that he shouldn't expect to have total recall of complex works of literature, philosophy, or theory. Nonetheless, he could keep a running journal of his ideas in the margin of the book or in a notebook. (By this time, I was convinced Brett had never learned any study habits.)

Brett accepted the idea of keeping a running journal of his ideas. When he first brought it in, he seemed genuinely pleased to show it to me. Often it contained interesting insights about the work, ones he was able to use later in class discussions and sometimes for essays. I saw no reason to comment on it and every reason simply to acknowledge his satisfaction. In short, I needed to stay out of his way while he took pleasure in what he was now able to do on his own.

In time, we accumulated a set of habits that worked for him: in addition to notes and a small planner, a routine of reviewing his notes and commenting in the margins on what seemed worth developing. For a biology class, he summarized his reading and lecture notes to make sure he was on top of the material. In tutoring sessions, Brett often viewed each accumulated habit as a new, important discovery for him. At times, we were able to hold animated conversations on his readings: a discussion of Kafka's *Metamorphosis*, a selection from Plato's *Republic*. Brett was trying out his ideas and enjoying it.

I didn't have to create much of a schedule for Brett, other than to suggest he e-mail me regularly about how his work was going, at first twice a week. By the end of the semester, he was working up to his potential, sure-footed about his abilities.

Brett's Needs

I view Brett's tutoring as another case of a tutor effecting a transition for a student, helping the student adapt to school when something has gotten in the way of doing so.

In Brett's case, what got in the way was his parents' divorce. Throughout my tutoring of Brett, I avoided conversation about it. For others, a divorce would not have been so disabling; for Brett it was, so I tiptoed around the topic.

And yet everything about his accumulation of study habits, his eagerness at discovering solutions to his faulty concentration, and his satisfaction at each achievement smacked of an adolescent becoming an adult—at least in academic terms. During the short amount of tutoring he required, Brett took over the full duties of caring for his academic life, which he'd been in the process of doing when his parents divorced. He needed a brief amount of tutoring to return him to that process. In effect, tutoring helped him to establish a connection to being in college. It did so by helping him with his study habits. It also did so because I was simply a presence in his education while he adapted.

Brett's circumstances aren't unusual. I could relate as well the stories of two students who moved to new high schools only to experience a brief difficult period of adjustment that caused them to withdraw from school for weeks. Tutoring helped them to catch up and to adjust to school while therapists attended to their underlying emotional issues. Still another student experienced a death in the family that brought on a period of academic difficulty. Tutoring helped the student to reestablish his abilities during this period. In each of these cases, a single incident brought on a temporary emotional difficulty; in turn, that difficulty led to trouble at school. Tutoring can have an enabling role to play in such circumstances.

A Summary of Possibilities

For Serena, Alice, Paula, Brett, Alexandra, and others who struggle with either chronic or short-term psychological difficulties, tutoring can help them move toward intellectual independence while a therapist furthers their emotional stability. Tutoring can therefore help them alter their beliefs that they cannot do the work of being a student. In all of these cases, tutors can fill a role that neither therapists nor the school itself may be able to perform. Therapists rarely have the time or the expertise to engage the student's work as does a tutor. The school simply doesn't have the resources or personnel experienced enough to work with such students. So there is a limited but truly important role that a tutor can play with students beset with psychological difficulties.

Tutoring students may raise a question for parents that is relevant for all kinds of students: Where does one find tutors to do this work? And are there good tutors to be found for everyone, regardless of income? The answers to these questions may be found in the final chapter, which is next.

CHAPTER SEVEN

Finding the Right Tutor

This final chapter advises parents on how to find a good tutor in their community. It guides parents on how to be resourceful in their search and argues that good tutoring should be available for everyone who needs it, not simply the wealthy and privileged.

So far, this book has urged you to adopt high expectations for the quality of tutoring your children receive. The tutor of your children should be someone who

- Connects easily and well with your children
- Scrupulously pursues the goal of making them comfortable and confident at meeting learning challenges independently
- Shows your children how they learn, so that they are wiser to what enables and what disables them
- Teaches your children constructive study habits and organizational skills
- Relentlessly pursues information from all sources to aid his or her ability to work with your children
- Is expert not only in the subject areas and skills being taught but also in the specific difficulties that challenge your children

These expectations are vital if tutoring is to play the transformative role for your child that it can—if it truly helps each child according to his or her unique intelligence. At the same time, these expectations may lead you to wonder where in the world to go to find tutors who have such standards and who fit the needs of your child.

How Parents Find Tutors

Locating a tutor is less difficult than it may appear at first; and parents should be assured that there are affordable options. Let's consider this process beginning with your recognition that your child is having some difficulties and may need the help of a tutor.

First Exhaust the Resources of the School

Before you spend your own hard-earned money, be sure to investigate whether your school has the in-house ability to help your child. Nearly every school has resident learning specialists, some with excellent training for working with learning difficulties, including learning disabilities. In many cases, however, school resources are stretched so thin that specialists don't have adequate time to devote to every child in need of tutoring. In my experience, with very few exceptions, learning specialists were available for each child for only a short period of time—twenty minutes to a half hour—and rarely as often as the child needs it.

If your child's problem is less difficult, it may be solved by extra time with a willing teacher or by peer tutoring. Teachers are almost always overcommitted, and peer tutors may be limited in their ability to help; but that is not always the case. Some teachers will find the time; some peer tutors are utterly wonderful in their abilities to help.

Using the resources of the school is not simply a matter of saving you money. It's also a way to teach your child to use what is around her to solve her problems. It's part of building intellectual independence and keeping your child connected to the school.

Then Define the Problem

Let's assume that you have exhausted the resources of the school. Your next move is to know what you're looking for to help your child. That requires an informed understanding of the difficulty he is having. Your understanding of your child's problem is unlikely to be precise. After all, the point of your looking for outside help is to investigate the difficulty and to resolve it as best you can. But if you identify the nature of the problem as well as you are able, you will save money that you might otherwise throw at solutions that aren't going to address your child's specific problems.

For example, to help your child with difficulties in algebra, you might hire a smart, amiable graduate student in mathematics from a local university. If you discover that your child has dyscalculia, however, you'll wish for someone experienced in working with this disability. If your child's difficulties in English, history, and Spanish derive from overall organizational problems or from ADHD, you'll want someone skilled and experienced in these areas rather than a tutor with expertise only in Spanish, English, and history.

Spend the time and if necessary the money to be clear about what is going on with your child. Assessing your child's needs may be as simple as consulting with his or her teachers or the resident learning specialists or counselors at your child's school. Or it may require having your child tested by a neuropsychologist—which is often helpful, but it's also costly. You can expect an experienced tutor to be good at assessing learning difficulties, but that doesn't replace the evaluations of others. Before you look for a tutor, you want to have a sense of where your child is struggling and why. Then you can search for a tutor whose expertise and experience fit the need. In some cases, the school may be able to refer you to a tutor. That is something I'll address later, where the chapter discusses who can help parents locate a tutor.

Avoid Tutoring Chains

Locating a good tutor is not about succumbing to the appeal of the most well-marketed, highest-profile businesses. Instead, it is like the search for a good doctor, dentist, lawyer, therapist, or piano teacher: you need to look in the right places.

Your goal as you search for a tutor is to find someone who can serve your child's unique needs rather than a company that supplies standardized tutoring help. There may well be a tutor working for a national tutoring chain who is able to do the job, but she will likely be forced by the protocol of the corporate operation into approaching your child in a formulaic way. The advantage of good tutoring is its ability to individualize help to fit your child's needs. A formulaic approach defeats that attempt. Some of the tutoring chains may offer more individualized help, but it will be considerably more expensive than their other services and often more expensive than individual tutors.

Resources for Finding the Right Tutor

This list of resources does not exhaust the possibilities, but it contains the most common ones parents use:

- Word of mouth
- Experts who can refer
- Private tutors or small tutoring companies
- Off-duty educators
- Local colleges and universities
- The Internet

The following discussion will help you evaluate each category for how it may be helpful and where you should proceed with caution.

Word of Mouth

Word of mouth is listed first because it is often the most powerful and persuasive way in which parents find tutors. A mother and father may readily praise the ability of a tutor who has worked well with their child, just as they will quickly warn you against the selection of a tutor who has disappointed them. Whatever the advice might be, you may feel a trust and confidence that you've found someone to consider or someone to avoid. And therein lies both the value and the problem with word of mouth: if you truly know the parent who offers advice on a tutor, you can gauge the value of the recommendation. It may be quite reliable—even more so, if this parent knows your child. If not, you may be relying on gossip alone.

A glowing endorsement, however, may not guarantee success. So much depends on the individual needs of your child and the personality fit between your child and the tutor. You may have heard stories of parents who highly recommend a tutor to work with another parent's daughter, only to find out later that the tutor didn't last more than two sessions. The parents may even know each other pretty well, and their children may be at the same school. It's easy to make a mistake like that. So be sure to ask yourself if these friends are insightful and intelligent regarding your child.

Strangely enough, word of mouth can sometimes cost you money. I know of extremely high-priced tutors who are in high demand in spite of their exorbitant rates because parents sing their praises. They have become trendy. Families flock to these tutors because they've heard they are "the best." In fact, they are good—if not very good— tutors, but there are others who would be just as excellent at far less cost.

Experts Who Can Refer

Professionals who work with children are excellent, reliable sources for referrals to tutors. Ideally, they should know your child; but even if they don't, they can often assess your child's difficulties swiftly and well. Moreover, many of them know reliable, good tutors to refer you to. A short list of professionals in this group include the following:

- Psychologists who provide neuropsychological evaluations, which include evaluation of learning abilities and behavioral difficulties such as ADHD
- Adolescent or child therapists—psychologists, psychiatrists, social workers
- Coordinators of learning services at your child's school
- School counselors
- Pediatricians and other physicians who specialize in child and adolescent medicine

Private Tutors or Small Tutoring Companies

Tutors and small tutoring firms also advertise themselves in the yellow pages and on the Internet. Some are excellent, have the area of expertise you seek, and are dedicated to comprehensive tutoring. If you go directly to private tutors, work backward from the tutor to those who know the tutor's work. Ask for professional references, check academic degrees, and ask questions to assure you of the tutor's expertise and experience.

Many tutors will have past affiliation or connection to schools, psychologists, or others who can vouch for their ability. If you can, seek out school counselors or child experts whom you know and ask them what they know about your potential tutor. Some tutors will be willing to put you in contact with the families of children they've tutored. Others will want to maintain the confidentiality of families with whom they have worked. For the reasons pointed out in the section on word of mouth, however, you may be better off focused on professional references.

Off-Duty Educators

Off-duty educators are also an excellent pool of caring, knowledgeable individuals whose expertise may fit the needs of your child. They include teachers, reading specialists, learning specialists, and school counselors who are doing freelance consulting and tutoring not connected directly to their day jobs. During the school day, they may not have the time to work extensively and regularly with your child; but after school may be another matter altogether. In many cases, psychologists and neuropsychologists use off-duty educators for tutoring referrals. For example, I know one excellent psychologist who refers students in need of tutoring for reading difficulties to specialists at a well-regarded elementary school.

Educators within your own school may be barred from tutoring your child. Many if not most schools consider it to conflict with the duties for which the educators are already being paid. But you won't have to look far. If it is acceptable and appropriate, ask educators at your school to direct you to either tutors or educators at other schools.

Contact reputable schools in your community to see if someone on their staff is available for this kind of work. As in all cases, the off-duty educator you consider should have the expertise that fits the needs of your child. If, for example, your child has a learning disability, say, dyslexia, there may well be a school that specializes in learning disabilities in your community, which would be filled with potential tutors.

Local Colleges and Universities

A comparable source of tutors may be in the colleges and universities of your community. The possibilities for where to search divide into three kinds:

- Departments focused on relevant subject matter
- Schools of education
- Learning services at the institution

Here again, whether you will find a potential tutor depends on the kind of difficulty your child faces. If the difficulty is specific to a subject—for example, math—then a department of math or math education may be a ready source of tutors. You're not looking for a professor willing to moonlight; you're looking for graduate students who might serve a similar function. Moreover, the department of psychology may have advanced graduate students who are experienced with behavioral or cognitive issues, if that is an important part of the problem your child faces.

You can contact the head secretary of the department and ask to be properly directed. Each department is likely to have a professor acting as director of graduate studies. A note of caution: finding a tutor for your child isn't the primary focus of these departments; not all of them will be open to such inquiries. But if they are willing to help, ask for referrals to graduate students who have shown particular ability as teachers.

Schools of education may be a more suitable source for graduate students who make excellent tutors. Departments that train students to work with learning disabilities, in reading, in counseling, and in teaching are all potential places for parents to find tutors.

The learning services at colleges may well include tutoring centers, writing centers, and support services for students with learning disabilities. They are there to support their own students, but they may have able people who are willing to tutor in the off-hours.

The Internet

No list of potential resources would be complete without mention of the Internet. From the Craigslist Web site to the Web sites of individual tutors and tutoring companies, the Internet provides an almost too-convenient means for connecting with people who offer tutoring services. Here again, the difficulty is in evaluating how credible the potential tutor is. Because the Internet is so open and inexpensive to use, nearly anyone can advertise tutoring services at a modest cost. Parents should be vigilant: check references carefully to convince yourself the potential tutor is reputable.

There are also online tutoring services. They offer individual tutors who chat directly with students and use *virtual blackboards* to communicate. For short-term difficulties with a particular concept or subject, these services may be useful. But these kinds of difficulties are likely to be addressed by peer tutors or in-school help. For more tenacious difficulties, these resources cannot substitute for full, direct, in-person contact and more comprehensive approaches to tutoring.

The Question of Expense

Until now, this chapter has said much about where to find tutors and only a little about how to afford them. There are no easy solutions here, and yet this book insists that good tutoring should be available to those students who need it, regardless of income. Like all aspects of quality education, tutoring should be an essential opportunity for every child and adolescent who needs it. Without that equal opportunity for all, we abandon the attempt to achieve democracy and equality in education; and we risk creating a population of youth who don't have the essential intellectual confidence to be active and responsible members of society. Tutoring should be available not simply for the wealthy but for everyone.

826 National and Other Nonprofit Help

Some nonprofit organizations have recognized as much, most notably 826 National, whose focus is exclusive to writing. This innovative organization provides free tutoring on writing in selected neighborhoods and in public schools of San Francisco, Los Angeles, Chicago, New York, Seattle, Boston, and Eastern Michigan (Ann Arbor, Ypsilanti, and Willow Run). Volunteers staff the various chapters of 826 National. There is also sometimes inexpensive tutoring offered as a community service through universities and colleges, through schools of education, and through selected institutions within the university, such as math labs.

And then there are long-standing nonprofits and volunteer organizations that are dedicated to providing individual tutoring and mentoring opportunities, especially for students in underserved communities. (These are not to be confused with the tutoring associated with the No Child Left Behind Act.) These organizations are found in virtually every city in the United States, from Nashville to Denver to Phoenix to Miami. They go by various names—Youth Encouragement Services, Tutor Mentor Connection, Tutor Corps. In addition, tutoring services are sometimes available through nonprofit youth organizations such as Boys and Girls Clubs. All of these may provide tutoring help of some kind.

In practical terms, however, there is no simple, comprehensive way to make tutoring available for all. Until the time when schools are able to afford tutors or more learning specialists to provide regular time with each individual student in need, the solution will have to come from the private efforts of tutors and parents. Making tutoring affordable to all will have to be addressed ad hoc—creating one method to make it affordable for one circumstance, another method for another circumstance.

Varying Fees

For tutors, making tutoring affordable for all requires them to be flexible about their fees and to volunteer in some cases. Tutors deserve to earn a fair wage for their work, according to their expertise and experience; but it's also reasonable to ask if they will work on a sliding scale.

This sliding-scale philosophy must work both ways. If parents ask tutors to adjust their fees according to the parents' ability to pay, they themselves will need to commit to paying as much as they can really afford. For some parents, the burden of providing for their children is already disproportionately large in comparison to the limitations of their income; so what they can afford will be small. For others, the fees for tutoring present less of a problem.

In my own practice, I have some students who pay full fee and others who pay essentially nothing. Nevertheless, I think it's important in most cases that the parent pay something, because a fee, however small, is often psychologically important: it's part of the commitment parents and students ought to make when pursuing lifelong career goals. And yet it should never become an insurmountable obstacle.

Establishing the Fee

When the care and development of your child is under consideration, money is often an uncomfortable subject. It is also an essential subject for parents and tutors to address up front. In many cases, when parents ask tutors how much they charge, the first answer they receive will be full fee. If so, and if money is an issue for your family, don't treat the tutor's response as a take-it-or-leave-it proposition. Take a deep breath and tell the tutor what you are able to afford. Imagine the appropriate fee as something to be negotiated between you and the tutor if the fee of the tutor is beyond your reach.

I understand the difficulty of being frank with a prospective tutor, especially one who you think would really be good for your kid. Stated bluntly, we live in a society that often equates success with your ability to pay. That makes it hard sometimes for parents to admit they aren't as wealthy as others. And yet you are in good company if you are of modest means. That company includes teachers, tutors, and professors, virtually all but a handful involved directly in the education of your children. No one does this work simply to make a living but also because they recognize the value of providing education for everyone.

Don't allow the subject of money to stop you from pursuing a tutor who may be an excellent fit for your child. The tutor may be able to take you directly or to tell you about someone else who is also a good fit but at a reduced rate.

I've frequently observed a kind of honor code, where tutors show flexibility about their fees and parents are honest about what they can afford. But even honor codes are occasionally broken. The parents of one of my students told me they had truly limited income. I charged them a considerably reduced fee, only to find out they lived on Park Avenue in New York and owned a vacation home in New England. They are the exceptions, however.

A Brief Survey of Fees

What exactly are those full fees? Of course they will vary. Let's look at some of the variables that affect fees before citing any general price ranges, which will change over the years. In this way, parents are more likely to be able to judge what to expect for charges.

Age and Experience of the Tutor

Let's begin with generalizations. You will pay more for age, experience, and ability. In most cases, a superior tutor will cost you more money, whether her expertise is in subject matter or in the nuances of learning styles and addressing learning difficulties. Parents shouldn't expect that a college student whom you pay $15 per hour will do work as good as someone with a graduate degree and years of tutoring experience. The experienced tutor, however, will be not just more expensive but also more responsible, more insightful, and therefore more transformative of your child.

All of these generalizations may be true, but so are the exceptions. I know of excellent, young tutors in New York who charge half the cost of others, for tutoring in some subject areas. These tutors are still unknown to parents or are reluctant to charge rates as high as other tutors until they get more experience. The adage "you get what you pay for" may to some extent hold, but not as strictly as some may wish.

Age of the Student

Some tutors will charge more for older students than for younger students. I know of tutoring companies that set their fees according to the experience of the tutor as well as the age of the student, whether in elementary school, middle school, high school, or college.

Region

Fees also vary by the region of the country, by the city, and even by the location within a city. To no surprise, the cost of private tutors is higher on the coasts than it is in the interior of the country. And it is higher in New York City than it is in Boston. In the more expensive communities within cities, the cost of private tutors also rises. It's what the market bears.

For example,

- Fees for tutoring in Chicago are generally less expensive than in Los Angeles and New York. Leaving aside the $10 or $15 per hour rates advertised in Craigslist, my brief survey found private academic tutoring fees in Chicago that included a low-end range from $20 to $30 per hour; a middle range from $50 to $75 per hour; and higher-end fees in the $80 to $90 per hour range—with a few tutors charging as high as $150 per hour.

- For Los Angeles, my survey found fees in the low end at $25 to $30 per hour; a middle range from $50 to $90 per hour; and a higher range from $100 to $150 per hour.

- There appear to be four ranges in New York City: the lowest fee range exists from about $30 to $40 per hour; a lower middle range from $75 to $110 per hour; and a middle to high middle range from $125 to $225. The fourth and highest range of fees is very high indeed: some tutors in New York City charge as much as $500 per hour for academic tutoring.

Those high prices are not a guarantee of excellence, nor are they representative of the average parents will pay. Parents shouldn't focus on the highest tutoring fees but on the norm—the math and science teacher with five years experience, now tutoring in St. Louis for $50 per hour, and for less in Des Moines. In every community, there are excellent tutors to be had at reasonable cost if parents look hard enough.

And excellence is the point, ultimately. If tutoring is done well, according to the unique intelligence and talents of each student, it has performed an invaluable service. It has helped students meet their learning challenges with confidence. It has helped free each student to develop his or her intelligence and talents, which will in turn make each of them more fulfilled and more active, able participants in society. Intellectual independence is a price worth paying for.

It's a goal to which I've dedicated my own work as a tutor, and I hope this book will inspire parents and other tutors to join me in this pursuit.

For parents and others who'd like to continue the conversation, I'd welcome hearing from you at james@jrmtutoring.com.

Books on Working with Students

Goldberg, Donna, and Jennifer Zwiebel. *The Organized Student: Teaching Children the Skills for Success in School and Beyond*. New York: Fireside Books, 2005.

Hallowell, Edward M., and John J. Ratey. *Answers to Distraction*. New York: Bantam Books, 1994.

Levine, Mel. *All Kinds of Minds: A Young Student's Book About Learning Abilities and Learning Disorders*. Cambridge, MA: Educators Publishing Service, 1993.

Levine, Mel. *A Mind at a Time*. New York: Simon & Schuster, 2002.

Stein, Judith, Lynn Meltzer, Kalyani Krishnan, and Laura Pollica. *Parent Guide to Hassle-Free Homework: Proven Practices That Work— From Experts in the Field*. New York: Scholastic Press, 2007.

Vail, Priscilla. *Smart Kids with School Problems: Things to Know and Ways to Help*. New York: Plume, 1989.

Whitley, Michael D. *Bright Minds, Poor Grades: Understanding and Motivating Your Underachieving Child*. New York: Perigee Books, 2001.

Books on Intelligence and Intellectual Development

Gardner, Howard. *The Unschooled Mind: How Children Think and How Schools Should Teach*. New York: Basic Books, 1995.

Gardner, Howard. *The Disciplined Mind*. New York: Simon & Schuster, 1999.

Gardner, Howard. *Frames of Mind: The Theory of Multiple Intelligences*. New York: Basic Books, 1999.

Healey, Jane M. *Endangered Minds: Why Children Don't Think and What We Can Do About It*. New York: Simon & Schuster, 1990.

Healey, Jane M. *Your Child's Growing Mind: Brain Development and Learning from Birth to Adolescence*. New York: Broadway Books, 2004.

Sternberg, Robert. *Thinking Styles*. New York: Cambridge University Press, 1999.

Books on Learning Difficulties and Emotional Difficulties That Affect Learning

Boylan, Kristi Meisenbach. *Born to Be Wild: Freeing the Spirit of the Hyper-Active Child*. New York: Perigee Books, 2003.

Kadison, Richard, and Theresa Foy DiGeronimo. *College of the Overwhelmed: The Campus Mental Health Crisis and What to Do About It*. San Francisco: Jossey-Bass, 2004.

Turecki, Stanley, and Leslie Tonner. *The Difficult Child: Expanded and Revised Edition*. New York: Bantam Books, 2000.

Books on Listening to Students

Cushman, Kathleen. *Fires in the Bathroom: Advice for Teachers from High School Students*. New York: New Press, 2005.

Karg, Barb, and Rick Sutherland, Eds. *Letters to My Teacher: Tributes to the People Who Have Made a Difference*. Cincinnati: Adams Media, 2006.

Pletka, Bob. *My So-Called Digital Life: 2000 Teenagers, 300 Cameras, and 30 Days to Document Their World*. Santa Monica, CA: Santa Monica Press, 2005.

Swope, Sam. *I Am a Pencil: A Teacher, His Kids, and Their World of Stories*. New York: Owl Books, 2005.

Inspirational Films and Novels on Teaching and Learning

Films

The Blackboard Jungle (1955)
The Miracle Worker (1962)
To Sir With Love (1966)
The Breakfast Club (1985)
Stand and Deliver (1988)
Dangerous Minds (1995)
Freedom Writers (2007)

Novels

Bincy, Maeve. *Evening Class*. New York: Dell, 2007.

Conroy, Pat. *Water Is Wide*. New York: Dial Press, 1987.

Konigsburg, E. L. *The View from Saturday*. New York: Simon & Schuster, 1998.

Web Sites

All Kinds of Minds. A nonprofit for assessing learning differences and bringing together educators, clinicians, parents, and students in the pursuit of accurate, helpful evaluation of learning difficulties. http://www.allkindsofminds.org/

826 National. A collection of nonprofits in seven cities rolled into one and dedicated to tutoring, instruction, and publishing students who are learning to write. http://www.826national.org/

Go City Kids. Provides parents with resources on tutoring and education in twenty-two cities in the United States. http://gocitykids.parentsconnect.com/

Professional Organizations for Evaluating Your Child's Difficulties

General Resources

American Academy of Child and Adolescent Psychiatry. http://www.aacap.org/

American Academy of Pediatrics. http://www.aap.org/

American Psychological Association. http://apa.org/

Resources for Specific Difficulties

Attention Deficit Disorder Association (focused on adults with ADHD). http://www.add.org/

Attention Deficit Disorder Resources. http://www.addresources.org/

Learning Disabilities Association of America. http://www.ldamerica.org/

National Center for Learning Disabilities. http://www.ncld.org/

National Dissemination Center for Children with Disabilities (NICHCY). http://nichcy.org/

ABOUT THE AUTHOR

James Mendelsohn, Ph.D., has been an educator for more than twenty-five years, at both the secondary and postsecondary levels. As a college professor, he has been visiting scholar in cultural studies at MIT, assistant professor of humanities and rhetoric at Boston University, and associate in the Department of African and African American Studies at Harvard University. He is a two-time winner of the Fulbright Lectureship in American Literature and American Studies, which he held first at the University of Tuebingen and then at the John F. Kennedy Institute for North American Studies, Free University of Berlin. In addition, he taught high school English at The Dalton School. He is the founder and principal of JRM Tutoring in New York City (http://jrmtutoring.com).

INDEX